S'cool Moves for Learning

Enhance Learning Through
Self-Regulation Activities

by Debra Em Wilson, MA and Margot C. Heiniger-White, MA, OTR

Copyright © 2000 S'cool Moves, Inc.
Illustrations by Penny Petrulis

All rights reserved. No part of this book may be used or reproduced in any manner, except for pages where instructions indicate the need to copy to implement the program. Brief quotations may be copied for reviews. The statistical data in appendix A may be copied to gather support for implementing the program as long as the authors are acknowledged.

This book is published by Integrated Learner Press

For ordering information:
Integrated Learner Press
P.O. Box 614
Shasta, CA 96087

Discounts available to schools and groups purchasing larger orders.

Library of Congress Catalog Card Number: 00-106630
International Standard Book Number (ISBN): 0-9706961-6-7

Fourth Printing..2008

Printed and bound in Canada by Hignell Book Printing

Cover design and desktop publishing by Debra Em Wilson
Data collection and evaluation by Debra Em Wilson and Doreen O'Donnell McClurg

For Your Information

The movement activities described in this book are for educational use only and are not intended to be a prescription for any ailment or medical difficulty. It is recommended that anyone using this program remain under the care of their medical professional. This program is intended to be used in an educational setting, or privately by assistants, parents, or guardians.

Dedication

Shalea and Daniel, my wonderful children, have deepened my understanding of the developmental process and its importance to learning.

Debi

Newell C. Kephart's teachings have been pivotal to my life's work. His concepts of kinesthesia, developmental sequence, perceptual and motor matching, and dimensions in space have stood in the foreground of my work with clients over the past 30 years.

Margot

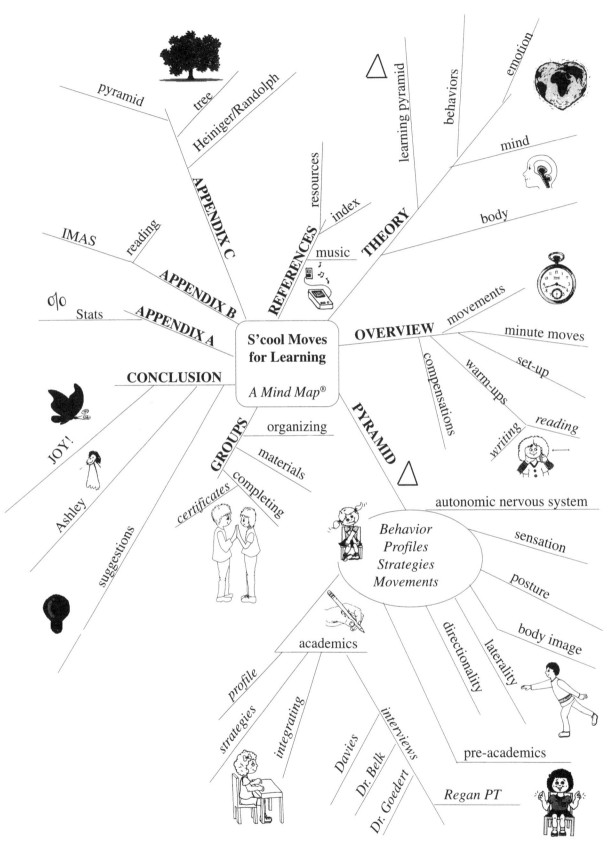

*Mind Map is a registered trademark of Tony Buzan as referenced in *The Learning Revolution.* Using mind maps instead of linear notes helps us remember the main concepts easier.

Table of Contents

Dedication		iii
Forward		ix
Acknowledgements		xi
Introduction		xiii

Chapter 1	**The Integrated Learner**	**1**
	The Movement-Learning Connection	2
	Chart of Behavior: Seeking Connections	6
	The Learning Pyramid: The Body-Mind Connection	12
	Dimensions of Space: The World Connection	20
	Bonding: The Emotional-Heart Connection	23
Chapter 2	**S'cool Moves for Learning: An Overview**	**25**
	Minute Moves for the Classroom	26
	Minute Moves Chart	27
	One Minute Warm-up for Reading	28
	One Minute Warm-up for Writing	29
	Tilling the Soil for Small Groups or Individualized Programs	30
	Referring Students	31
	S'cool Moves for Learning Referral	32
	Program Development	33
	Developmental Sequencing	33
	Observing Compensating Behavior	34
	Integrating the Auditory, Visual, and Kinesthetic Systems	36
Chapter 3	**The Small Group Design**	**37**
	What is Needed for Small Groups and Individualized Sessions?	38
	Incorporating Small Groups into the Daily Routine	38
	Individualized Programs	40
	Organizational Tips	40
	Completing the Program	40
	Certificate of Participation	42
	S'cool Moves for Learning Summary Chart of Movements	43
Chapter 4	**Autonomic Nervous System (ANS)–Survival Systems: Setting the Foundation for Learning**	**45**
	Chart of Behavior Review: ANS–Survival	46
	Student Profile: ANS–Survival Level	47
	Strategies for Success: ANS–Survival	48
	Movements for the Teacher and Students	50

Chapter 5	**Sensation: Processing Information Through all the Senses**	53
	Chart of Behavior Review: Sensation	54
	Student Profile: Sensation	55
	Strategies for Success: Sensation	56
	Integrative Movements and Activities	57
Chapter 6	**Posture: Balance and Muscle Tone Needed for Academics**	63
	Chart of Behavior Review: Posture	64
	Student Profile: Posture	65
	Strategies for Success: Posture	66
	Integrative Balance Movements	68
Chapter 7	**Body Image: Staying Centered While the World Around Us Changes**	75
	Chart of Behavior Review: Body Image	76
	Student Profile: Body Image	77
	Strategies for Success: Body Image	78
	Integrative Movements and Activities	79
Chapter 8	**Laterality: The Internal Sense of Having Two Sides of the Body that Work Separately and Together**	83
	Chart of Behavior Review: Laterality	84
	Student Profile: Laterality	85
	Strategies d for Success: Laterality	86
	Integrative Movements and Activities	87
Chapter 9	**Directionality: Knowing the Left From the Right and Other Directional Terms**	99
	Chart of Behavior Review: Directionality	100
	Student Profile: Directionality	101
	Strategies for Success: Directionality	102
	Integrative Movements and Activities	104
Chapter 10	**Pre-Academics: Integrating the Auditory, Visual, and Kinesthetic Systems for Learning**	105
	Chart of Behavior Review: Pre-Academics	106
	Student Profile: Pre-Academics	107
	Strategies for Success: Pre-Academics	108
	Auditory-Visual-Motor Activities	111
	Vision Activities	112
	Eye-Hand Coordination and Visual-Motor Activities	115

Chapter 11 **Academics: Putting All the Pieces Together** 119
      Student Profile: Academics 120
      Strategies for Success: Academics 121
      Integrating Academics into S'cool Moves for Learning: A Matter of Creativity 122
      Tying up Loose Ends—Talking with Specialists 125

Chapter 12 **Conclusion: Some Final Thoughts** 137
      Ashley's Story 138
      Building a Solid Learning Foundation at Home and School 142

Appendix A **Statistical Data 1995–2000** 145
      School Demographics 146
      Program Design 146
      School Improvement Program (SIP) 147
      Title I 149
      The Integrated Motor Activities Screening (IMAS) 151

Appendix B **The Integrated Motor Activities Screening (IMAS)** 157
      Using the IMAS to Compliment Reading Programs 158
      IMAS Student Data Summary Chart 161
      Relationship of IMAS Items to the Learning Pyramid 162
      IMAS Assessment Items and Classroom Implications 163

Appendix C **Margot Heiniger and Shirley Randolph's Work** 167
      The Tree of Learning 168
      The Pyramid of Learning 169

Chapter Reference Notes 171
References 174
Learning Resources 177
For More Information 178
Music Selections 180
Index 182

Forward

What a joy it is for me to see this work finally arrive in printed form. The fateful meeting of Margot and Debi created the perfect path for this book to be written—and what a joyful book it is—honoring children's unspoken needs, and creating a place for them to grow through movement. The movement activities and interventions described in this book balance the body, mind, and emotional systems allowing children to make the essential connections necessary for creative and stress-reduced learning.

This project is a result of over thirty years of nurturing, caring, and seeking answers for children with special needs. During that time, Margot Heiniger-White developed and refined the "Learning Pyramid," the foundation upon which this book stands. Debi Heiberger's collaboration with Margot has produced a practical, use-friendly reference that any teacher or related service provider can utilize. If you are a teacher who is concerned about students who have difficulty staying focused, performing to potential, self-organizing, or who seem out-of-sync in the classroom, this book is for you.

One of life's gifts came to me when I discovered Margot Heiniger and Shirley Randolph's Learning Tree Seminars. As a young therapist seeking answers for children with special needs, it was there I first learned to connect the behavior I was seeing with the underlying neurophysiological causes. Those principles have formed my life's work as a physical therapist working with children with sensory integration difficulties, autism, and physical challenges. As a consultant for public school systems, I have experienced firsthand the effectiveness of giving foundational support to children. The results have produced self-motivated and confident students.

S'cool Moves for Learning gives us a meaningful tool to successfully apply the movement-learning connection within the classroom. What joy there is for teachers to discover the underlying factors limiting their students' potential, and turning frustrating situations into positive learning opportunities. In order to solve a problem, one must first understand it. This book helps the user identify and understand possible causes for learning difficulties in the classroom.

The movement activities described are organized in a way that is easy to integrate into the class routine throughout the day. The Minute Moves for the Classroom, included in several chapters of this book, is a handy reference of movement activities which help make transitions from one activity to another fun and smooth. These activities invite students to improve their focus in preparation for reading, writing, math, spelling, and test-taking.

My wish is that you will feel empowered through the content of this book to discover the hidden potential within each of your special children, and experience daily the happiness children bring to our lives.

Freddie Ann Regan, Physical Therapist

Acknowledgments

We owe a debt of thanks to the children, parents, colleagues, friends, and family members who have supported us along our journey. Sharon MacKenzie, a retired principal and superintendent, provided a safe haven and encouragement for the beginnings of *S'cool Moves for Learning*. We thank the teachers and paraeducators who created an environment where the culmination of Margot's life's work was brought to fruition. We appreciate the encouragement, support, and wisdom of Norma Bowers, Joyce Brady, Susan Holthaus, Doreen McClurg, Sharon Potter, Lisa Saulsbery, Linda Michaels-Spivey, Anna Steele, Betty Stiliha, Les Wilson, Elaine Woolley, and Blaine Yoho.

Steve Heiberger patiently assisted Debi with the overall design of the book, offering an artistic eye for consistency, detail, and accuracy of the drawings. Brenda Morris thoroughly edited the book and provided us with expert advice on writing style.

We are grateful for the talents of Penny Petrulis, residing in Illinois, who illustrated our cover and completed drawings for the book between teaching kindergarten and going to her three sons' baseball and basketball games. Special thanks to Morgan Harman and Rachel Seguin for being our models for the drawings.

We thank Dr. Judith Belk, Dr. Steven Goedert, and Freddie Ann Regan, PT for contributing to the academic chapter of this book. Freddie Ann's insight throughout the book made it more complete. We reference other talented people and acknowledge their contributions to the field of education. Debi personally acknowledges Elizabeth "Liz" Davies, one of the original perceptual-motor training pioneers who worked with Newell C. Kephart, and served as one of Debi's mentors.

Margot acknowledges Shirley L. Randolph for their twenty plus years of working, writing, and teaching together. Shirley's studies and training increased Margot's awareness of Margaret Rood's work, especially her presentation of developmental sequence. Shirley and Margot's partnership was dedicated to working and teaching their combined areas of knowledge to severely physically challenged clients, as well as children and adults with attention and hyperactivity difficulties.

Introduction

"I think that all mind patternings are expressed in movement, through the body. And that all physically moving patterns have a mind. That's what I work with."

Bonnie Bainbridge Cohen
Sensing, Feeling, and Action

We were brought together on this project through a series of interesting coincidences which resulted in an occupational therapist and a teacher merging their perspectives on how children become physically, emotionally, and intellectually ready for school. We have blended our two fields together and designed a movement program that meets the needs of children who have underlying factors affecting their ability to learn, and as a result, are struggling to keep up with their peers in an academic setting.

We have directed this book toward teachers. In a broad sense the term "teacher" could include anyone who guides children through the learning process—parents, physical and occupational therapists, counselors, doctors, and professionals working in some way with children. The words in this book will be filtered through each individual's personal and professional experience. We have provided the foundation for people to process and apply this information within their frame of reference, making the material uniquely their own.

The original intent for this book was to use it during our inservices, workshops, or seminars. As we shared the initial outline with people, many suggested we present the material in a way to make it possible to use this program without any formal hands-on instruction from us. Readers who have a background in body-mind theory may understand exactly where we are heading. We encourage readers who have not been introduced to the literature discussing the body-mind connection to further explore the references we have provided for a broader perspective of the principles touched upon in the chapters ahead.

When we began working together on this project, our discussions often focused on answering the question, "When do learning difficulties begin?" Our conversations covered a wide range of possible answers to this question. One area of particular interest for both of us was the possibility that a child's incomplete developmental patterns may contribute to later learning challenges.

From the very beginning of a child's life, the learning process unfolds. In the womb, the fetus is emotionally connected to the mother and interacts with his womb environment. The birth and early developmental experiences become the foundation for real world learning. The way infants and toddlers interact with their environment determines how their real world learning will transfer to learning in the school setting. Through involvement in creative play and activities that develop the body-mind system, children refine the skills needed for academic learning. We explain our reasoning in chapter 1, The Integrated Learner.

Chapter 1 provides our readers with theory to understand how the uterine, birth, and developmental processes create the underlying foundation for a child's emotional security, physical stability, and academic success. We have shared a story about Grace, a young child who received many different medical opinions to explain her developmental difficulties—none of them accurate.

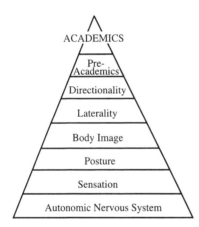

The Learning Pyramid

We worked with Grace and used movement experiences, like those discussed in this book, to help her fill in the missing movement patterns that kept her from fully participating in activities second nature to most children. Grace, now four years old, is back on track and meeting all the normal milestones. We relate Grace's difficulties to behavior children exhibit in the classroom setting. The Learning Pyramid is a simple visual diagram to show how behavior is related to stress, sensory processing difficulties, weak muscle tone, poor balance, gross or fine motor difficulties.

We chose to use a light hand when discussing body-mind science knowing this field is moving at a rapid pace, and new discoveries are making headlines almost daily. There is marvelous information currently available through recently published books, on-going brain research, and via the internet.

Chapters 2, 3, and 4 discuss how to use S'cool Moves for Learning in the classroom, with small groups of children, or on an individual basis. The movement activities in chapters 4 through 11 fit within each of the Learning Pyramid levels and are designed to improve factors contributing to problems children have in the classroom. The chapters profile different children having difficulty at each level of the pyramid and include strategies to support children in the classroom setting.

Chapter 11 focuses on how to integrate academics with movement. We tie up loose ends by interviewing specialists knowledgable in areas that frequently give children problems: writing, listening, reading-related vision difficulties, and behavior concerns.

This is an exciting time to work with children. Body-mind science offers fascinating ways to improve learning for all children. The neuroscience field has just begun to apply its ever-expanding wealth of knowledge to children in the classroom. The specialists interviewed are on the forefront, using the latest blend of science and technology to improve learning for students struggling to meet the standards and testing requirements dominating today's educational system.

The concluding chapter profiles Ashley, a first grade student who completed an individualized S'cool Moves for Learning program. Ashley attended the same school through her eighth grade year which enabled us to follow her progress. It is an inspiring story, and one of our most enjoyable to share. We keep our conclusions brief and end with some simple suggestions to enhance the development for children at home and school.

Appendix A provides statistics showing students' performances in reading and math at an elementary school in rural Northern California between the years of 1995–2000. During this time, the elementary school began using the Integrated Motor Activities Screening (IMAS), developed by Margot Heiniger. Children scoring low on the IMAS and having learning difficulties were involved in S'cool Moves for Learning, along with participating in a powerful, coordinated reading program. The success of the students was due to many factors: paying attention to neuro-physiological difficulties, research-based teaching practices, strong staff training in reading, dedicated staff, parent involvement, supportive administrators, and open-minded school board and site council members.

For readers currently using the IMAS, appendix B provides information about using the screening as part of an early intervention reading program, and discusses ways to use S'cool Moves for Learning to improve children's scores on the IMAS.

S'cool Moves for Learning

Margot Heiniger and Shirley Randolph's Pyramid of Learning and Tree of Learning are in appendix C for easy reference. The two diagrams are from their book *Neurophysiological Concepts in Human Behavior*. The book was a textbook for physical and occupational therapists.

The reference section includes literature to deepen your understanding of the theory presented in this book. Many talented people and creative programs contributed in some part to the whole of S'cool Moves for Learning. The "For More Information" section serves as a resource for those who want to contact individuals or organizations dedicated to providing quality educationally-related services for parents, students, and teachers.

If we have done our job well, we have piqued our readers' curiosity and willingness to try the movement activities and strategies in this book. Turn to chapter 2 and refer to the Minute Moves Chart to see how easy it is to integrate movement into the academic areas in minutes throughout the day. Integrative movement is a wonderful way to start the day, and creates a place where teachers and their students are energized, focused, and ready for a great day! Adding music to the program during classroom participation incorporates another dimension and is fun for children. At the end of the reference section, we have included songs that lend themselves to the different movements. Music can calm or energize. Choose selections that are appropriate for the learning activity.

Whether using integrative movement with your whole class, or starting a more ambitious small group or individualized program, the brief amount of time spent daily with movement activities will enhance the learning environment for all children in the classroom setting.

Chapter 1

The Integrated Learner

- The Movement-Learning Connection
- Chart of Behavior: Seeking Connections
- The Learning Pyramid: The Body-Mind Connection
- Dimensions of Space: The World Connection
- Bonding: The Emotional-Heart Connection

"Long before a child ever reaches school age, he has begun to learn. His learning began at his conception and should continue to grow in unison with his body throughout his natural life...Both brain and body work together..."

Sally Goddard
A Teacher's Window Into the Child's Mind

The Integrated Learner

This chapter provides the theoretical support for S'cool Moves for Learning. The movement-learning connection begins in the womb. Once outside the womb, the baby continues her remarkable growth and discovers daily how to move in new ways, working toward smooth, coordinated movement. We share the story of Grace, a young child who missed learning key movement patterns and consequently struggled with daily activities second nature to most children. Grace's difficulties are related to behavior patterns seen in school children, and lay the foundation for the movement activities used in S'cool Moves for Learning. The reference section of this book provides titles of books that cover this material in greater depth.

The Movement-Learning Connection

The movement-learning connection begins in the womb as the fetus interacts with the mother. A living being's environment is always in a state of dynamic balance. This is true for the fetus in his internal environment, the womb, or for the infant in his external environment, the outside world.

All living beings have an innate sense of survival. When a baby is born, his first experiences in the world communicate to him whether the world is a safe place or a fearful place. His view of the world will set in motion his innate survival response, manifested in one of two ways. If the baby feels safe, loved and secure, he will move toward growth, feeding, and interacting with the people and things in his world. If the baby feels that the world is a stressful, threatening place, he will move away from growth and activate protective survival responses that will cause him to withdraw and shut down. The survival response begins in the womb and plays a major role in the baby's feelings of safety or stress.

Insight from literature focusing on the womb environment offers a unique perspective on the importance of the womb experience in creating the foundation for how the infant bonds, interacts, and learns once outside the womb.[1] According to Dr. Bruce Lipton, a cellular biologist, the infant brings with him, into the world, the experiences and feelings he had in the womb. Dr. Lipton's studies focus on how genetic and environmental factors contribute to human development and behavior. From his studies we learn that the mother acts as the interface between the fetus and his outside world. The fetus is learning to move in response to the mother's emotions which stimulate the chemical systems shared by the fetus and the mother. In the womb, the fetus is learning that he is safe and free to grow and interact with his environment, or he is learning that life is threatening and he must withdraw and protect himself. In the process of withdrawal, the foundation for learning through continual experience within the womb is limited, and may lead to developmental difficulties after the baby is born.

Sharing a true story about Grace, a little girl that we had the pleasure to work with, demonstrates this process. We met Grace's mother during a seminar in Oregon. We began working with Grace when she was 22 months old. Grace, though a beautiful, loving, and happy child, had feeding difficulties, limited speech, weak posture, and did not interact well with her environment. People often commented on what a "good baby" she was. Her mother, father, and pediatrician were concerned that she was not growing and thriving as she should.

Grace's parents were well-educated and had purposely waited to have a child until after establishing solid careers. The mother took excellent care of herself during the pregnancy. She ate well, kept her prenatal appointments, completed sonograms, and rested when needed. However, there were stressful events that the mother had no control over. She had contracted a virus in the first trimester that put her in bed for a week. During her second trimester, the mother's family experienced several personal tragedies that increased the mother's stress level. She began to experience severe back pain that was aggravated when she moved.

Feeling better, while in her last trimester, the mother chose to continue working through her last month of pregnancy. She began her pregnancy leave a week before her due date. Grace was born, two weeks past her due date, after her mother experienced an induced labor that was long, difficult, and stressful. The baby's birth weight was six pounds and eight ounces.

The first few days after her birth, Grace was unable to suck at the breast. After prolonged feeding periods, with minimal amounts of milk consumed, she would fall asleep exhausted from the energy expended while attempting to suck. Grace refused to suck on a bottle, so the mother continued breast feeding, feeling this was the best way to nourish her.

Grace cried when she was placed on her stomach, and showed neck weakness when attempting to lift her head up. Due to Grace's strong objection to being on her stomach, she was placed on her stomach for only brief periods of time. The parent's awareness of Sudden Infant Death Syndrome added to their hesitation to put their daughter on her stomach. The SIDS research suggests that infants should be placed on their sides or backs while sleeping. Parents are misinterpreting the SIDS recommendations and placing their babies on their backs, not only while sleeping, but during the active part of their days, as well. Grace missed out on critical tummy time during her awake periods that would have improved her neck and torso strength, sensation, and posture. Grace was taken to many doctors and specialists to help determine the cause of her poor growth and overall slow developmental progress. Different medical opinions were offered, with none fitting her situation.

We spoke with Grace's parents about the possible connection between her utero stress and birth experience as underlying the lack of development. The parents were open to exploring ways to help their daughter heal her prenatal and birth traumas. To determine the exact reason for Grace's struggles would be impossible. We proceeded with the parents in an atmosphere of genuine concern and trust.

The first step in healing for Grace was to have her comfortably curled in the fetal position where she could feel safe and close to her mother in a peaceful way. Initially, she would kick her legs straight out and not allow herself to be put in the fetal position. We suggested the mother hold her while taking a bath together. Grace began to adjust to being held in the fetal position in the water and started enjoying the experience. Within a few weeks she accepted being curled in the fetal position out of the tub, and tolerated it for longer periods of time. To improve her feeding difficulties, her mother improved the sensation to Grace's lips and tongue area through deep pressure stimulation, (discussed later in this book).

Grace's feeding began to improve as she discovered how to properly use her tongue and lips to eat.

Grace missed the belly crawling stage and went right into creeping on hands and knees, pulling to stand, and walking at eighteen months. Her fine motor skills were exceptional for her age, appearing before gross motor competency and out of developmental sequence.

At 24 months, the parents discovered that Grace had hearing loss due to continual ear infections. Her hearing loss was in the critical range at which children hear language sounds. Hearing loss during the first two years of her life contributed to a delay in language development. After weighing options, the parents decided to have tubes placed in her ears and worked with a holistic health practitioner to remedy the causes for her ear infections. Grace's hearing returned to normal levels, and she no longer experienced ear infections. Her interaction with the world improved, though she continued to have gross motor coordination problems, weak torso muscles, and language delays.

After discussing Grace's progress with her parents, we added whole-body deep pressure stimulation to the program to enhance her ability to take in information from the environment.[2] Within one month, Grace was able to sit up while going down a slide, something she was unable to do prior to the deep pressure stimulation. Her torso strength increased and her coordination began to show major improvement. Grace continued to do a series of movements similar to those found in this book, to fill in her missing developmental pieces. At age three, her gross motor coordination was age-appropriate.

Due to earlier oral motor and hearing difficulties, Grace still had a language delay and would not risk speaking freely to people unless she knew them well. Though developmental and cognitive tests showed her to be in the normal to above-average ranges, she chose to sit back and observe rather than be an active participant in the world. We advised the parents to take Grace to see Dr. Judith Belk, a specialist in listening therapy (see chapter 11 for more information). Grace began a listening program to improve her vestibular-auditory systems' ability to process and organize sound and language.

At four years old, as a result of continued listening and speech therapy, Grace communicated with others and used language as a form of personal power. Her speech and motor planning skills still showed signs of lagging behind her peers, despite a lot of improvement. At age 5, a sensory integration evaluation determined that Grace would benefit from sensory integration therapy, a form of therapy that focuses on the vestibular system and other sensory systems of the body. While participating in therapy, Grace became more active and developed a stronger sense of self. Motor planning, speech articulation, tactile sensation, and dominance all improved dramatically. Grace's ability to track and use her eyes for literacy tasks remained a challenge. She began balance-auditory-vision exercises (Bal-A-Vis-X) to prepare her for school. Grace's parents elected to enroll her in a Montesorri program where she could work at her own developmental level, become more independent, and be challenged without undue stress.

Throughout her young years, Grace was involved in a modified form of S'cool Moves for Learning designed to help her move through the survival mode and improve her ability to take in and process information from her environment. Strengthening posture created the foundation for her to continue developing fluid, coordinated movement. She shows all the normal signs of emergent literacy including using a dominant hand for drawing and scribbling, interacting and questioning as she is read stories, and pretending to read to other children. Grace is a delightful child who is loved by her friends for her warmth and easy-going personality. Through movement and interaction with people and things in her world, Grace is building the foundation for future academic and social success. What happens to children who have not been fortunate enough to work through their early emotional and physical challenges? Children's academic, emotional, and behavioral problems in the classroom could relate to early unresolved challenges similar to Grace's difficulties.

Chart of Behavior: Seeking Connections

The Chart of Behavior on the following pages, was developed from workshops with teachers who consistently reported the behavior on the charts as those observed most frequently in their students. In schools, we rarely take into account uterine, birth, or developmental history. Children show up at the school door on the

---

Behavior We See in Our Students

Squirms all over
Sloppy posture
Bugging other kids
Tense pencil grip
Messy writing
Eyes close to paper
Slow to start
Spaced-out

chart found on the next page include the elements of the Learning Pyramid: Autonomic Nervous System (ANS)–survival systems, sensation, posture, body image, laterality, directionality, and pre-academics. To use the chart, select the behavior of concern and note which columns have an "x" in them. For example, if the sensation and posture are marked, turn to those chapters in the book for a full discussion of the movements that will help alleviate the behavior of concern by strengthening sensation and posture.

Behaviors may be listed under different elements of The Learning Pyramid. For example, awkward pencil grip appears under sensation, posture, laterality, and pre-academics. If this is the case, design a program for the child that incorporates movements from each of those chapters beginning with the lowest level (sensation). Remember, though The Learning Pyramid is a linear, sequential model; children are working on all elements (some areas more than others) throughout the course of their development.

It is important to acknowledge that observed behaviors as those reported on the Chart of Behavior receive diagnosis as varied as Attention Deficit Hyperactivity Disorder (American Psychiatric Association), Sensory Integration Dysfunction (Ayres), learning-related visual problems (Kavner and Cook), nutrition allergies (Rapp, Crook, and Smith), or may merely be the characteristics of a normal child (Gesell).[3]

The best approach with children who consistently exhibit these types of behavior is a sensible, multi-disciplinary, developmental approach that treats underlying causes rather than the secondary symptoms. A community of multi-disciplinary experts, including members from the medical, behavioral, and holistic health care professions need to be available for parents and teachers to consult. S'cool Moves for Learning is most successful when community experts, parents, teachers, and the child come together to discover and remedy the factors beneath the behavior.

Chart of Behavior and Likely Underlying Physical Causes

A full discussion is found in...	Chapter 4	Chapter 5	Chapter 6	Chapter 7	Chapter 8	Chapter 9	Chapter 10
Behavior Demonstrated	ANS	Sensation	Posture	Body Image	Laterality	Directionality	Pre-Academics (A-V Motor)
aggressive: physical and verbal	x	x					
arms disappear in clothing	x	x					
awkward pencil grip		x	x	x	x		x
bizarre verbal outbursts	x	x	x				
cannot sit still	x	x	x	x	x		
clothes-sucking and shirt-turning	x		x				
clumsiness		x	x	x	x		
constantly needing to use the bathroom	x						
covers one eye; work placed to one side		x			x		
does not finish work	x		x			x	x
difficulty forming letters and numbers					x	x	x
easily distracted	x	x	x				
everything is boring	x	x					x
face on top of paper		x			x		

8

Chart of Behavior
and Likely Underlying Physical Causes

A full discussion is found in...	Chapter 4	Chapter 5	Chapter 6	Chapter 7	Chapter 8	Chapter 9	Chapter 10
Behavior Demonstrated	ANS	Sensation	Posture	Body Image	Laterality	Directionality	Pre-Academics (A-V Motor)
falls out of chair			x				
humming noises		x	x				
hyperactivity	x	x	x	x	x		
inappropriate self-touching	x	x	x				
itchy eyes	x	x					
knee-sitters and chair-rockers	x	x	x	x	x		
lacks eye contact	x	x	x	x			
no paper hold while writing		x	x				
off-task	x	x	x				x
pencil chewing	x	x	x				
perfectionist or non-risk taker	x	x	x				
reversal of letters or numbers					x	x	x
sitting on edge of chair			x		x		
slow starter			x				x

9

Chart of Behavior and Likely Underlying Physical Causes

A full discussion is found in...	Chapter 4	Chapter 5	Chapter 6	Chapter 7	Chapter 8	Chapter 9	Chapter 10
Behavior Demonstrated	ANS	Sensation	Posture	Body Image	Laterality	Directionality	Pre-Academics (A-V Motor)
spaced-out	x	x	x				
speech difficulties	x	x	x				
stressful reading	x	x	x		x	x	x
tears	x	x					
tension and stress from home or school	x						
tongue helps out during tasks		x	x		x		
trouble with boundaries	x	x	x	x	x		
whole body lays on desk			x		x		
wraps legs around chair			x		x		
writing from bottom-up				x	x	x	x
writing very light or dark		x	x				x
writing on one side of paper					x	x	
writing very small, large, uphill, downhill		x	x	x	x	x	x
writes with no space between words			x	x	x	x	x

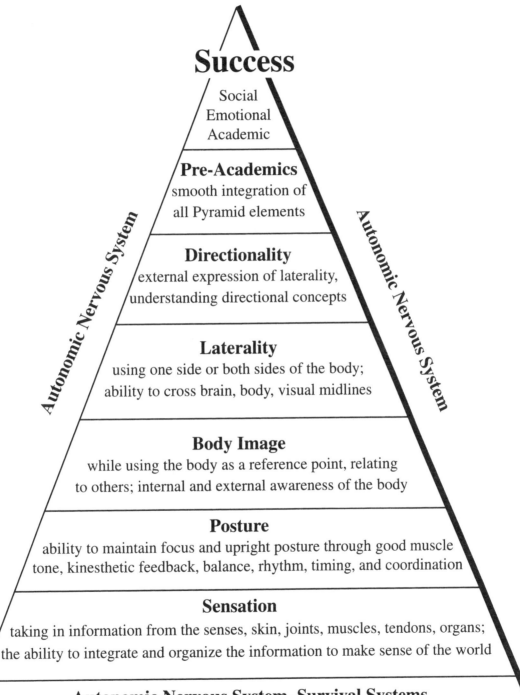

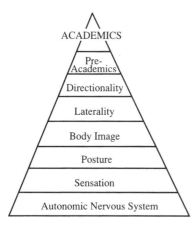

The Learning Pyramid

The Learning Pyramid: The Body-Mind Connection
Bonnie Bainbridge Cohen said it well when she stated, "In order to speak of a totality of being which does not dichotomize body and mind, one ends up using two words which do (body-mind)."[4] Candace Pert, Ph.D uses the term bodymind in her book, *Molecules of Emotion*.[5] She discusses the science behind mind-body medicine and explains that our emotions link the two together. As the physical and emotional factors in our body change, the mind changes. As the mind changes, the body responds in turn. It's quite a fascinating process, indeed.

The Pyramid of Learning was first presented in the book *Neurophysiological Concepts of Human Behavior: The Tree of Learning* written for occupational and physical therapist (see appendix C).[6] The description of the pyramid elements were changed using terminology common to the educational field. To reflect the changes, the Pyramid of Learning was renamed the Learning Pyramid. The Learning Pyramid is a concise and simple way to build a theoretical foundation for the movement activities in this book. Though the Learning Pyramid depicts a sequential developmental process, the elements are interwoven, repeated, and expanded at each level. In this chapter, each level of the Learning Pyramid is briefly discussed. The reference section provides titles of books covering this information in greater depth.[7,8] Chapters 4 through 11 discuss the movements that improve body-mind communication at each level of the Learning Pyramid.

Autonomic Nervous System (ANS)–Survival Systems: Setting the Foundation for Learning
The autonomic nervous system includes the sympathetic nervous system and the parasympathetic nervous system. Both systems play distinct roles in the survival of human beings. The sympathetic system ensures survival by providing a quick response to anger, fear, or threat of injury. The parasympathetic system is the peacekeeper, helping the body regain balance and harmony when faced with a life-threatening or extremely stressful situation. The parasympathetic system promotes growth, a sense of safety, and feelings of well-being.

Arousal levels undergo normal variations throughout the day. For most children, there is a dynamic balance between the sympathetic nervous system and the parasympathetic nervous systems. When both systems are operating in sync, thinking and actions are balanced. If the balance on the continuum is tipped toward either end, there will be physiological signs to help determine which system is not balanced.

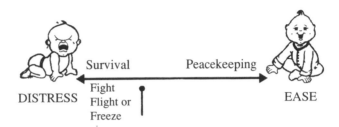

If a child has gone into the "shut down" mode and is not communicating verbally, watching body language can help determine how the child is responding to his environment. If the sympathetic system is aroused, specific physiological changes take place in the body. These changes include dilated pupils, increased heart beat, increased blood pressure, increased respiration, cold and clammy sweat, or thick saliva indicating a stopping of digestive juices. The muscle tone is tense, and peripheral vision is activated, indicating that the child is on the lookout for danger and must be ready for fight or flight. Sometimes the child will choose neither fight or flight, and just freeze. When the child freezes, there is no verbal communication and motor planning ability is impaired.

If the parasympathetic system is aroused, there will be physiological signs including a slowing of the heart beat, decreased blood pressure, shallow respiration, warm and wet sweat, and constricted pupils. The muscles will be relaxed and the child will appear to be calm and mellow.

Children experiencing difficulty maintaining a balance between the sympathetic and parasympathetic systems may exhibit a variety of behavior ranging from anger and aggressiveness (fight), to withdrawal, daydreaming, mellowness, or no focus (flight or freeze). Physiological and behavioral indicators can be used to clarify whether a child is over-aroused and in sympathetic shut down, or under-aroused and in parasympathetic lethargy. Understanding which end of the ANS system is unbalanced provides a way to determine strategies to use with the child to balance the two systems. Arousal levels in a child affect behavior in the classroom. The key to success is to attain the "just right" arousal level for the activity at hand.[9] For example, lower arousal levels are more necessary while doing seat work than for competitive physical education games.

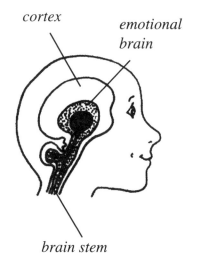

cortex *emotional brain*

brain stem

The brain plays a role in determining arousal levels. Simply put, the brain stem's role is to ensure survival by maintaining unconscious body functions and preparing the body for a fight, flight, or freeze response to threat and recovery from perceived threat. The emotional brain is responsible for regulating emotion and storing long-term memories. It can override rational thought and innate brainstem response patterns. The cortex receives, categorizes, and interprets sensory information, makes rational decisions, and activates behavioral responses.[10] The cortex, emotional brain, and brain stem must communicate with one another to maintain balance of the ANS. For example, if a child is stressed, the brain stem may be overactive, reducing the emotional connection to learning and higher level processing. With appropriate movement, the ANS stress response is reduced, allowing for the emotional brain and cortex to function properly. Integrative movement improves learning by maintaining communication and developing all parts of the brain (see chart at the end of this chapter).[11]

We discuss strategies to keep the ANS balanced in chapter 4 and provide a closer look at the role the autonomic nervous system plays in the classroom by including an interview with Freddie Ann Regan in chapter 11.

When we look back at Grace's early life, we recall that she was experiencing difficulty balancing her two survival systems. Grace was not sucking properly, often appeared under-aroused, experienced slow growth, and delayed development. The uterine and birth stress put Grace into an extreme survival mode causing her autonomic nervous system to remain in a state of imbalance. Grace received new information about her world through deep pressure stimulation, close holding in the fetal position, and providing her with a safe, loving environment. New information from her outside world changed what was going on inside her. Learning took place at the basic body level. She regained balance with the autonomic nervous system and began to thrive.

Sensation: Processing Information Through all the Senses
Most people think of sensation as the five main senses of seeing, hearing, touching, tasting, and smelling. There are many more sensations in the body that affect a child's behavior and responses to her environment.

Kinesthesia or kinesthetic awareness are two words used interchangeably to explain how the body uses sensation to provide information about the world. Kinesthesia includes the sense of touch, an internal sense of body position from muscles and joints, and gravitational sensation. The easiest way to explain kinesthesia is to demonstrate it. While putting one hand behind the back, make the hand into a fist (tension), and then open the hand back up (relaxation). Curl it into a fist again, and then open it back up. With the kinesthetic sense, one knows that the hand is behind the back and what the hand is doing. There is no need to look behind the back and look at the hand to make it do the movement. In all daily activities, kinesthesia provides the foundation to plan our movement. This sense is located in the muscles, joints, tendons, and ligaments of the body. Muscles and tendons give information about posture, balance, gross motor activities, and coordination of our body parts. Through sensory neurons, the brain receives continuous messages about where the body is in space and time, discussed later in this chapter. Another quality of kinesthesia includes the ability to sense light touch and pressure. Both of these types of touch are necessary to handle tools such as pencils, crayons, and scissors, and to do manipulative activities with the fingers.

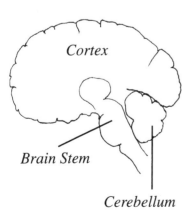

Cortex

Brain Stem

Cerebellum

The vestibular system is a nerve-system centered in the brainstem and linked very closely with the cerebellum and the inner-ear mechanism.[12] The vestibular system connects through the vagus nerve to the sympathetic and parasympathetic systems. Vestibular sensory input is related either to motion or position of the head in relationship to the force of gravity. Without the appropriate orientation to gravity, normal development is disrupted. The vestibular system coordinates all sensory motor impressions into a coherent understanding of the world. The body's orientation in space, ability to balance, and coordinate gross and fine motor activities are all under the direction of the vestibular system. It influences and provides the foundation for efficient functioning of the sensory system and the autonomic nervous system.

Grace was experiencing difficulties with sensation causing her to eat poorly, have limited interaction with her environment, and move in an uncoordinated fashion. She over-used her visual system to compensate for her inability to hear well. The lack of sensory experience would continue to limit her development, had she not received intervention.

Posture: Balance and Muscle Tone Needed for Academics
Muscle tone, balance, kinesthetic feedback, timing, and coordination are the foundation for good posture. Posture is dependent on information that is constantly fed back and forth to our muscles. The muscle groups—flexors and extensors—work in opposition to one another. While one set of muscles contract, the other set relax, creating smooth and coordinated movement.

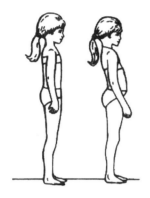

The child on the left is exhibiting good posture. The child on the right is exhibiting weak posture.

The foundation for posture is laid when a baby is developing the flexors and extensors of the body through movement in utero, and after birth while lying on his stomach. In utero, through fetal flexion in the last trimester, babies develop their fetal position which activates all the flexor muscles necessary for good posture. Infants who spend a lot of time on their stomachs while lying, preferably, on a hard surface, will develop the strong extensor muscles necessary for adequate posture later in life.

Children who compensate for posture difficulties may begin a task with "all engines, go" and then fatigue before completing the task. As the activity becomes more complex and requires increased concentration, the energy demands become too high and fatigue posture sets in. When the child must put a lot of energy into posture and balance, there is little energy left for higher level skills like reading and writing.

Let us look at Grace's development as she attempted to develop posture. She disliked being on her stomach because lifting her head against the force of gravity was a lot of work. Her mother was hesitant to put Grace on her stomach because she often cried. Also, she was concerned about SIDS. Developing posture while on her back was impossible. Her over-reliance on the visual system created a need for her to be on her back so she could see what was going on around her. Missing key movement experiences including flexion, prone extension, and belly crawling created a lack of postural strength soon evident when she was unable to sit unsupported and unable to maintain a sitting posture while going down a slide. Walking and other gross motor activities were also delayed.

Body Image: Staying Centered While the World Around Us Changes
Body image is a child's awareness of who she is, using the body as a reference point to judge other relationships. Body image includes body concept and body scheme. Body concept is the conscious naming of body parts and understanding their functions. Body scheme is an unconscious, internal awareness of the body and its function.

All lower levels of the Learning Pyramid, including ANS, sensation, and posture, must come together for a child to have a good body image. Though parents may build confidence and provide their children with positive feedback about their bodies, children may not have good body images if they do not have body scheme.

Children with poor body image may have difficulty naming body parts, be unable to sit still, lack eye contact, appear clumsy, hold onto other children, and irritate others by not honoring personal space and boundaries.

As children strengthen the lower levels of the Learning Pyramid, their body image improves. A child who is insecure and unwilling to try new things may become more confident and begin to enjoy taking risks. In Grace's case, as she began to gain control of the lower level Learning Pyramid elements (sensation and posture), she started to reach out to others around her and interact with her friends. She became more confident in her abilities as demonstrated in her desire to dress herself and do things on her own, without her parent's help. She began to have opinions, sharing her likes and dislikes with her family. The child who was once an observer became an active participant in this wonderful experience called "life."

Laterality: The Internal Sense of Having Two Sides of the Body that Work Separately and Together
Laterality is the internal awareness of the two sides of the body working together and in opposition. Babies begin developing

laterality by using the two sides of the body together, as seen in a baby who is propping himself up with both arms so he can raise his head. Soon the baby learns to use the sides of the body in opposition to do two different things: one side is propping up the body while the other side is reaching for a toy. As the child develops and experiments with using the two sides of the body, a preferred or dominant side emerges. The child learns how to move one part of the body without moving other parts.

Laterality includes the ability to cross the midline of the body. One midline intersects the two parts of the body, separating the top and the bottom of the body. Another midline intersects the body at the center of the left and right sides of the body. A third midline divides the body from front to back. Dr. Newell C. Kephart, one of the leading experts in perceptual-motor development, and author of numerous books on the subject referred to the three midlines as "dimensions of space." [13] Midline difficulties may be observed in children by watching how they function within the different dimensions of space.

When observing the use of hands, midline problems are seen in a lack of a preferred hand, using both hands for a job that requires just one, or turning the body to avoid crossing the midline. Sometimes children will begin writing with one hand and then switch hands at the midline to avoid crossing over the midline, or they may be unable to write and hold the paper at the same time. When observing the use of the legs, midline problems are seen in a lack of preferred leg, inability to balance on one leg, hop, or skip. The eyes may not smoothly track across the midline of the body, or the eyes and head may move at the same time. Some literature expands the definition of laterality to include the communication between the right and left hemispheres of the brain.[14, 15]

Directionality: Knowing the Left from the Right and Other Directional Terms
Every day you witness children involved in directionality experiences. Watch three year olds in action. One of their favorite things to do is dress and undress themselves. This fun activity is helping them discover their preferred side, and develop directional concepts such as right and left, in and out, above and below, or inside-out and right-side out. Watch a toddler maneuvering his

body as he crawls under a stool, climbs on top of a chair, and moves in and out of the cupboards. While playing with his toys, he puts things on the shelf, takes them off the shelf, and puts them back on again. He stacks his blocks, knocks them all down, and stacks them up again. He is naturally involved in dynamic play that will teach him the concepts of directionality.

As laterality and directionality become more developed, children begin to use the terms "left" and "right"—usually at about age eight. Laterality and directionality are the foundations for recognizing the difference between "d" and "b", or "was" and "saw." Children must have directionality concepts to place numbers in columns and align words neatly on a page with appropriate spacing. During reading, directionality is essential for the eyes to smoothly scan the page from left to right. During dance and movement activities, directionality is needed to stay in step with the other children.

Pre-Academic: Integrating the Auditory, Visual, and Kinesthetic Systems for Learning

The pre-academic level of the Learning Pyramid is where the child strengthens and integrates the lower levels of the Learning Pyramid. The pre-academic level includes the integration of hearing, visual perception, auditory discrimination, visual memory, articulation, and auditory- and visual-motor skills. It is important to observe children as they enter into the pre-academic phase. Some children have developed their gross and fine motor skills and are ready to begin writing and other academic tasks. Children who are not ready will show signs of frustration that lead to compensating behavior such as awkward pencil grip, covering one eye while reading, and maintaining body tension. Proceed cautiously when children show compensating behavior and provide movement opportunities that help develop their physical foundation for learning.

Academic: Putting all the Pieces Together

The peak of the Learning Pyramid is the academic level. At this level children have integrated the lower portions of the Learning Pyramid and are able to maintain control of their bodies, organize themselves in space, and communicate using the visual, auditory, and kinesthetic systems.

Dimensions of Space: The World Connection

To function in the world, children must develop a system for organizing themselves. Because there are no absolutes or reference points in the environment, the infant must develop a system for dealing with spatial and time relationships, once outside the womb. There is nothing in the human nervous system that gives direct information concerning space. Space is a learned phenomenon based on the interpretations of sensory information. The most direct clues about space come from body movement through kinesthetic receptors located throughout the body.

Euclid's spatial system is the most frequently used system to explain how children organize themselves in space. There are three dimensions of space which include the vertical, horizontal (lateral), and transverse (fore and aft). The fourth dimension of space is time, which is defined as the stopping of movement in any of the three dimensions of space.[16] How children function in the classroom is related to their internal understanding of Euclidean space. To put this simply, a child who seems to be everywhere in the room may have a poor concept of where he is in space, therefore he is always part of his environment and never a separate entity within the environment. He does not understand how to organize his movement so that he knows where he is in space and time. Children who do not have an internal sense of space and time need to get their information from the environment. They need constant reminders to focus, keep their hands to themselves, and give others space. They exhaust and frustrate the people around them. Children who have organized themselves in space are connected to the world and remain centered, though the world around them is in constant flux.

In the vertical dimension, gravity pulls the child toward the earth in a constant direction. The baby's first job in life is to work against the force of gravity with the goal of eventually achieving a standing position.

movement in the vertical dimension

The body's stability begins with holding the head upright, against the force of gravity. Development continues as the child's movement patterns become more complex and he begins to push himself up onto his forearms, crawl on his belly, sit, creep on hands and knees, kneel, and eventually stand upright. Movement experiences at all levels help the child coordinate the top and bottom of the body. The child learns and internalizes the concepts of up, down, above, and below.

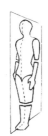

movement in the horizontal or lateral dimension

As the vertical dimension develops within the child, the horizontal or lateral dimension is also developing and relates to gravity in a slightly different way. The child learns to recognize the distance from the spine (body's midline) to the ends of the extremities. This new-found internal measuring device begins from side to side movement and develops stability in the lateral plane.

As laterality develops, the child learns to move the same two sides of the body together in a bilateral pattern. As the child begins to integrate both sides of the body, he learns how to move his limbs in opposition to one another. A child who exhibits well developed laterality uses both sides of the body together or separately as needed to accomplish a task. The laterality dimension is the foundation for understanding the concepts of left and right within the body, and naming left and right outside the body (directionality).

Some authors theorize that there is a relationship between lateralization of the body with lateralization and integration of the two hemispheres of the brain.[17, 18, 19, 20] Lateralization of the brain is observed in a child who integrates both hemispheres of the brain. For instance, the child uses the logic hemisphere to decode words, and the gestalt hemisphere to comprehend what is read.

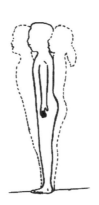

movement in the transverse dimension

The transverse dimension begins at the center of the body and progresses forward and backward. Eventually, this is how we "divide the world" into front and back. This is also the foundation for depth perception. The force of gravity is intimately involved with the development of muscles and stability of the body. Balance is regained every time the body moves in a bending forward, straightening up, or moving backward position.

The fourth dimension of space is time. All movement in the three dimensions of space have an element of timing (rhythm, pace, and sequence). Rhythm involves fluency, smoothness, and stable intervals in time. Rhythm occurs in the human body and is present in blood and lymph flow, circulation, digestion of food, and respiration. Coordination of muscle actions give the body posture and stability as it rhythmically completes movement patterns of crawling, creeping, and walking. There is also rhythm involved when taking in visual, auditory, and kinesthetic information through the sensory system of the body.

Pace is a way of altering the time component without disrupting rhythm. A rapid pace relates to small intervals, closer together, and a slow pace relates to large intervals, further apart. There may be an even or uneven pace while maintaining rhythm.

Sequence provides an organization in the time dimension. All movement involved in learning is sequenced. Some children do not develop the dimensions of space and time within their bodies—rhythm, pace, and sequencing may be difficult. This is observed in the classroom where children seem to be one step behind or out of step altogether. When a child is integrated and moving smoothly within the dimensions of space, the foundation for learning is solidly in place. Current science validates the connection between rhythm and timing to focus and attention.[21]

Bonding: The Emotional-Heart Connection

The emotional-heart connection is the bonding that takes place between a child and the significant people in her life. The first and foundational emotional-heart connection is the bond between the mother and her fetus in the womb. This connection develops the baby's earliest feelings of safety, love, and acceptance. The second connection is between the mother, father, guardians, or caregivers who provide food, shelter, and a safe environment outside the womb. While developing emotional ties to loved ones, the infant deepens her trust and understanding of the world as a warm and safe place to grow and thrive.

When children enter school, the emotional-heart connection is extended to their teachers, significant adults, and peers. Children are very sensitive to their environment and intuitively know if it is safe to take risks, and when they are supported during their learning experiences. Learning is most powerful when children make the emotional-heart connection with others who nurture their growth. Researchers in the field of neuroscience have discovered that the emotional component of learning needs to be addressed first and foremost for children to reach their ultimate learning potential.[22, 23, 24, 25]

Children are motivated and focused learners when they relate at an emotional level to information presented. The emotional connection includes feeling safe to explore the curriculum through questioning, discovery, and applying their findings to the real world. If children are threatened by their learning environment, the emotional brain shuts down higher level processing essential for long-term memory and critical thinking.

Movement described in this book balances the body-mind and emotional system so that children make the essential connections necessary for creative, joyful, and stress-reduced learning.

How physical activity builds a child's mental abilities

What a child does *physically* in the first few years of life plays a major part in how well he or she will develop other abilities. Here's a simple model of how it works:

1. The instinctive reptilian brain	The activity: Grasping Touching Crawling Arm-leg Walking movements Reaching Pushing Turning Pulling	Leads to: Hand-eye coordination Big-motor skills Prewriting ability
2. The balancing cerebellum 	The activity: Spinning Tumbling Balancing Dancing Listening Swinging Rolling	Leads to: Balance Sporting ability Bicycle riding Writing skills Fine motor coordination Reading skills
3. The emotional brain	The activity: Stroking Cuddling Playing together	Leads to: Love Security Bonding Social skills Cooperation Confidence
4. The thinking brain or cortex	The activity: Stacking toys Assembling puzzles Recognizing patterns Making patterns Playing word games Repetitive play Appreciating music	Leads to: Math, logic Problem solving Fluent reading, spelling Writing, painting Good vocabulary Memory Musical ability

Special thanks to Gordon Dryden for encouraging us to include this chart in the book. Reprinted with permission from *The Learning Revolution*. Originally reproduced from *FUNdamentals Guidebook,* by Gordon Dryden and Colin Rose.

S'cool Moves for Learning

Chapter 2

S'cool Moves for Learning: An Overview

- Minute Moves for the Classroom
- Minute Moves Chart
- One Minute Warm-up for Reading
- One Minute Warm-up for Writing
- Tilling the Soil for Small Groups or Individualized Programs
- Referring Students
- S'cool Moves for Learning Referral
- Program Development
- Developmental Sequencing
- Observing Compensating Behavior
- Integrating the Auditory, Visual, and Kinesthetic Systems

"There is something in nature that forms patterns. We, as part of nature, also form patterns. The mind is like the wind and the body like the sand; if you want to know how the wind is blowing, you can look at the sand."

Bonnie Bainbridge Cohen
Sensing, Feeling, and Action

S'cool Moves for Learning: An Overview

Minute Moves for the Classroom

For teachers who want to get moving with their students in the classroom, the next three pages provide Minute Moves that can be done throughout the day, in literally minutes! We have included a handy reference chart highlighting movements to improve focus and prepare students for reading, writing, spelling, math, and test taking.

Each of the movement activities is covered in the chapters ahead. A big part of a teacher's job is maintaining discipline and focus. The movement activities on the following pages require very little time and reduce the amount of time and energy a teacher spends disciplining and getting students to pay attention.

Teachers can learn how to read the body language of children and change behavior by changing the environment and choosing the appropriate movement for the desired energy level. When students are over-energized for reading, writing, and math, reduce the high energy level and improve focus by Deep Breathing (chapter 4), Deep Pressure Stimulation (chapter 5), Figure 8's on paper (chapter 8), Listening Ears (chapter 10), or the One Minute Warm-ups for Reading and Writing (following pages).

When children need to wake-up and become more energized, offer movement opportunities that involve large muscle groups such as Cross Crawls (chapter 8), Rhythm Tapping (chapter 4), Partner 8's (chapter 7), or Sit and Pats (chapters 4 and 10).

Teach children how to self-monitor their energy levels so they can choose the appropriate movements and find their "just right" activity level. Encourage children to notice when the class needs specific movements to calm or energize all students.

> *All classroom movement activities are designed to fit into the school day whenever there is a minute or two!*

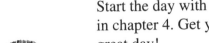

Minute Moves Chart
Copy this page and keep it as a handy overview of how to integrate the movement activities within academic areas, in minutes! If there is a leader for the day or week, he can be responsible for leading movement throughout the day.

Morning Moves in Minutes
Start the day with munchies, music, mind, and motion as described in chapter 4. Get yourself and students focused and energized for a great day!

Before Reading
Offer body-mind integration movements including Figure 8's (chapter 8), Palming (next page), Deep Breathing (chapter 4), and One Minute Warm-up for Reading (next page).

Before Spelling
Sing while spelling words and doing Listening Ears (chapter 10), Sit and Pats (chapters 4 and 10), or Cross Crawls (chapters 4 and 8).

Before Writing
Prepare the hand and mind for writing by guiding students in Figure 8's, Squiggles (chapter 10), Paper Crumpling (chapter 10), OK's (chapter 10), or One Minute Warm-Up for Writing.

Before Math
Count, recite, or sing math facts while doing Sit and Pats or Cross Crawls.

Before Art or Music
Have the whole class do the Developmental Symphonies 1 or 2 (chapters 5, 6 and 7) while playing slow beautiful music.

During Physical Education
Get the most of P.E. time by adding any movement in this book.

Before tests, including standardized achievement tests
Have all students drink water to hydrate the brain, do Rhythm Tapping, Figure 8's on paper, Listening Ears, One Minute Warm-ups for Reading and Writing, Deep Breathing, and end with Cross Crawls to integrate all the movements.

One Minute Warm-Up for Reading

When children and teachers move their eyes, they access different parts of the brain, strengthen their eye muscles, and even relieve stress! One simple way to get the eyes moving and warmed-up for reading is to follow this simple one minute procedure. Students use their thumbs or the erasers of their pencils for this activity. Adding a sticker to their thumbs or cute eraser top to pencils helps improve tracking.

Convergence: Have the children bring their thumbs or pencils straight in toward the nose to a comfortable point; not too close. Move the pencil in a downward arc away from the nose, at arm's length. Repeat three times. Reverse the movement and have the children move their thumbs or pencils away from the nose and then in a downward arc toward the nose.

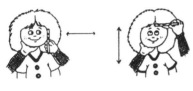

Side to Side and Up and Down Tracking: Have the children move their thumbs or pencils at eye level from the left side to the right side, and from the right side to the left side. Repeat three times. Have the children move their thumbs or pencils up and down at the midline. Keep the elbow straight to maintain a comfortable distance. Repeat three times.

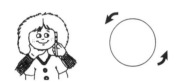

Circular Tracking: Have the children move their thumbs or pencils clockwise in a circle once, and counterclockwise once, keeping within a comfortable field of vision.

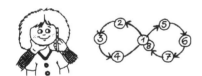

Figure 8's: Have the children move their thumbs or pencils in the Figure 8 pattern, at arm's length, and then again with the elbow bent for near and far focus.

A nice way to end the reading warm-up is to have children do some palming. If time is of the essence, children may skip palming and get right to their reading.

Palming: Have the children rub their hands together until the palms are warm, then gently cover their closed eyes with the palms of their hands. Overlap the fingers above the bridge of the nose to create as much darkness as possible. Keep the eyes covered for a minute or two. Add deep breathing. Palming revives the eyes, warms the hands for writing, and quiets the mind.

One Minute Warm-Up for Writing

Teachers often notice children having difficulties with the physical components of writing: pencil grip, wrist movement, staying in the lines, forming letters, and overall legibility. One Minute Warm-up for Writing was compiled from an interview with Freddie Ann Regan, PT who works with children struggling in the classroom with numerous difficulties, including writing. This warm-up improves the physical skills needed for writing and is used to improve focus when students are too energetic.

Deep Pressure Stimulation: Have the children press the thumbs of each hand into their opposite palms. Press deeply and firmly all over the palms. Next, squeeze the forearms, upper arms, and shoulders by crossing the arms over one another and squeezing the right side with the left hand, and the left side with the right hand.

Skin Sensation: Have the children rub the palms of their hands together, the backs of their hands together, and rub in-between their fingers. Clap the hands loudly. Pat the forearms and shoulders. Have the children give themselves a pat on their backs.

Muscle Sensation: Have the children pretend to put on their writing gloves. These are very long, tight gloves. Pretend to put the glove on the writing hand. Pull the glove up to the shoulder with firm pressure strokes. Repeat several times. Be sure to get out all the wrinkles in each finger of the glove.

Resistive Pressure: Have the children push their palms together. Next have them grasp their fingers together at chest level and try to pull them apart. Have the children pat their hands on the desk and rub the desk. If Figure 8's are drawn on the desk, children can rub the pattern.

Joint Compression: Have the children press their hands into the desk. Next, press the hands into the thighs trying to press the feet into the floor.

Writing Posture: Have the children sit up tall with their feet firmly planted on the ground. The paper is placed at a slight angle to the midline of the body. "Righties" tilt their heads slightly to the left, and "lefties" tilt their heads slightly to the right. Review correct pencil grip (chapter 10).

Tilling the Soil for Small Groups or Individualized Programs

For those who would like to develop a small group or individualized program to target specific children having academic difficulties due to weak physical foundations, start with this chapter and read each chapter sequentially. Developing a small group or individualized program requires laying some ground work before getting started.

The very first step is to validate the powerful movement-learning connection that affirm integrative movement programs are an effective way to improve learning (see references for supporting literature). Share your findings with other interested folks in your professional circle. If you decide to proceed, inform your principal/superintendent, school site council, and the school board of your interest in developing a movement program for your students. The school system, site council, and school board approval of S'cool Moves for Learning is essential to ensure proper information goes home to parents and the community at large. Set the ground work firmly in place to avoid misinformation going out to parents and the community.

Small groups require twenty to thirty minutes per day, depending on how many children are participating. Working with individual students takes fifteen to thirty minutes per day. The key to success is daily, consistent sessions with the children.

Parent permission slips should be signed for all children participating in small group or individualized programs. As part of the permission slip, include a brief description of the program and invite parents to "drop in" whenever they want to observe. Better yet, meet individually with parents and encourage them to come to school and learn the movements so they can follow through at home.

This program includes some touching to demonstrate movement activities. When there is a need to touch a child, be sure to ask the child for approval. A simple question such as, "May I show you where to put your arms?" is very effective at relieving anxiety in the child and ensuring his personal space is honored. If a child resists being touched, move forward with non-touching activities until the child develops trust.

Referring Students

We recommend there be specific reasons for referring children to participate in the movement program. When children are referred, state goals explicitly in written form so growth can be measured. Setting goals with the child, parent, and teacher's input helps build a mutual understanding of why the child is participating in the program and clearly identifies expected outcomes.

When selecting children in grades K-2, we recommend using the Integrated Motor Activities Screening (IMAS), developed by Margot Heiniger (see appendix B for details), though any assessment may be used as a beginning benchmark for students. If there is not enough time for a complete IMAS, or if children are in grades higher than second grade, see appendix B for Margot's quick one-minute gross motor evaluation. Set a benchmark for vision tracking as well as gross and fine motor skills. The referral on the next page may be used for children of any age, or tailored to meet specific needs. It is important to check the areas of concern and write clear goals for the students entering the program.

There is limited time throughout the regular school day to spend assessing children. School districts have staff psychologists who assess for special education services and provide information to the parents and teachers about specific areas covered in psychometric tests. It is not the intention of this program to assess children with the types of tests designed to be used by specially trained personnel. The suggestions provided in a S'cool Moves for Learning program are simple, quick, and informative without crossing the line into areas that teachers are not trained to assess.

Using a starting benchmark such as having the child draw a self-portrait (see chapter 7) or geometric forms (see appendix B) is a way to measure change in body image, laterality, and fine motor control as the child progresses through the program. Periodically, have the child draw another self-portrait or redraw the geometric forms to monitor progress. Obtaining an entry-level writing sample or reading fluency rate also serves to measure change. Progress is rapid if the program is well designed for the child. If a month has passed with no observable signs of positive change, review the child's program and make adjustments.

**S'cool Moves for Learning Referral
Check the Items of Concern**

Academic

____ Writing _____
_____
_____

____ Reading _____
_____
_____

____ Math _____
_____
_____

____ Spelling _____
_____
_____

____ Reversals_____
____ Vision tracking difficulties or head tilted to one side
____ Overall difficulties _____
_____
_____

Behavior, Social or Emotional

____ Lacks gross or fine motor coordination
____ Distractable or lacks focus
____ Unmotivated, low muscle tone, or too mellow
____ Agressive, angry, or difficulty getting along with others
____ Sensitive to touch and textures
____ Excessive movement, fidgeting, and squirming
____ Blurts out in class, interrupts, or impulsive
____ Acts young for age
____ Poor listening skills
____ Other:_____
_____

Goals for the program: _____
_____
_____
_____
_____
_____

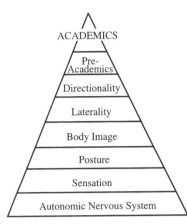

Program Development

After choosing students to participate in S'cool Moves for Learning, the fun begins! Knowing where to start is relatively easy.

Chapters 4 through 11 discuss the Learning Pyramid, starting in sequential order with the Autonomic Nervous System and working up the pyramid to Academics.

When in doubt as to where to begin with a child, begin with the information in chapter 4 to balance the ANS and ready the child for learning. Proceed to the movements outlined in chapter 5—the earliest developmental patterns in the program. Children may work in more than one Learning Pyramid level at the same time. For example, a child may work on sensation, posture, and body image in the same session.

It is important to work with students every day for maximum benefit. However, not all activities need to be completed every day. Alternating activities keeps interest high and alleviates the stress of trying to get everything done each day.

Children who are given a lot of new information through integrative movement *and* academics may become overloaded. When children receive intense reading support on a one-on-one basis, schedule their movement sessions to complement their reading instruction. At the end of each movement session, it is very important to have a few minutes of time for the child to quiet himself and transition to the classroom environment.

During the beginning weeks of the program, children may exhibit negative behavior as they integrate newly learned information about their bodies and reorient themselves with the world. Sometimes children become angry, sad, quiet, clumsy, or silly. They may do worse academically or socially. Within a couple weeks, these children begin to show positive changes and continue to improve in their ability to complete movement activities in each of the Learning Pyramid levels.

Developmental Sequencing

It is important to understand the developmental sequencing of the integrative movement activities in chapters 4 through 11 so children do not develop splinter skills. A splinter skill is any task done using tension, uncoordinated movement patterns, or sheer will to complete the task. There is a normal developmental pattern that evolves when learning new movement patterns. S'cool Moves for Learning offers movement patterns in a developmentally sequential manner so movements are integrated and do not become splinter skills.

Floor level activities are the starting point for movements in this program so children do not have to work against gravity as much as they would sitting or standing. Movement in the standing position requires good balance, therefore, for most activities, doing them at the standing level would be more difficult than lying down or sitting. For example, a child can usually do Cross Crawls while lying down. If the child has balance difficulties, she will have a difficult time doing Cross Crawls while standing.

Let us apply the knowledge of developmental sequencing to skipping. For a child to skip in a fluid manner, the child must know how to jump with both feet, balance on one foot while standing, and hop on either foot. Children who cannot walk up and down stairs using alternating steps will have difficulty balancing on one foot and hopping on one foot. Teaching the child to skip before mastering jumping and hopping will create an awkward skipping pattern. If there is a pattern at all, it will be in the form of a rigid gallop without alternating arms. Skipping would then be considered "a splinter skill." For this reason, jumping with both feet, hopping, and finally skipping are introduced in the appropriate developmental order in the laterality chapter.

This same line of thought holds true for most new concepts children learn. For instance, teaching children to write using their large motor skills while standing at an easel or sitting on the floor transfers efficiently and easily to writing at a desk using fine motor skills. Writing, while in a sitting position, requires more energy than standing due to high level integration skills in the areas of sensation, posture, balance, laterality, and directionality.

Observing Compensating Behavior

In the classroom, children are challenged when asked to do things out of developmental sequence. As a result, children will compensate to get the job done. Compensating behavior comes in all sorts of creative ways including, but not limited to, an awkward pencil grip, a rump sticking up in the air while kneeling on the chair, paper pushed to one side of the desk, or one eye covered by a hand while reading. Often it is helpful for the child to "backup to move forward."[1] Backing-up to move forward takes the child to a place where support at his or her developmental level provides growth in a progressive manner and reduces the chances of developing splinter skills. Sometimes a child is not making the desired progress with a certain movement and the assistant does not know why. The clever child may have devised a way to perform movement through compensating behavior. It takes careful observation to realize when a child is avoiding the true essence of a movement. Sometimes the child's avoidance is very subtle and yet, no growth occurs. Each movement description in the following chapters includes a detailed explanation of possible compensating behavior observed as children attempt the movement. If you suspect a child is compensating, it is best to question the student rather than fall into a pattern of "gentle nagging."

Correcting Compensating Behavior
Instead of telling the child to change what he is doing, it is more effective to ask the child, "What do you notice about how you're doing this movement?" or "What do you need to fix?" or "Wow, that's an interesting way to do that. Why do you do it that way?" Usually, children are the last to be asked and the first to know why they do what they do. It's often quite logical. For example, a teacher kept giving students lessons on capitalization because they continuously capitalized in the middle of sentences. Finally, frustrated and beaten she asked the students why they were not getting it. They replied, "Oh, we know how to capitalize, we just don't know which way our b's, d's, and p's go, so we use capital letters instead." *Before* all else fails, ask the child.

Support
It is important to reinforce the positive behavior you observe. Statements such as, "I like the way you...", "How does it feel now that you've corrected...?" and "Every day you get smoother" goes a long way in gaining cooperation and affirming positive changes.

Self-Evaluation
Ask the child, "How did you do today?" "What was difficult?"

"What was easy?" "What is getting easier for you?" "What changes do you notice in your reading, writing, or school work?"

Integrating the Auditory, Visual, and Kinesthetic Systems

To ensure that a child does not develop splinter skills and fully integrates the auditory, visual, and kinesthetic systems require the child to listen, talk, and do some vision tracking while completing the movement. First, make sure the child can do the movement easily, without compensating behavior. The child listens to the assistant while keeping the movement pattern fluid. If this is done easily, ask the child questions and encourage a response. The movement patterns should remain fluid at all times.

The greatest challenge is integrating the visual system. The assistant moves an object in a Figure 8 pattern in front of the child's eyes while he is doing a movement such as Robo-Pats. The assistant's fingers or fist may be used for tracking. Tracking while doing the movement is difficult for the child, initially, but becomes easier with practice.

The highest developmental activities are found in the academic area of the program (chapter 11). Literacy or math skills are introduced while the student is doing movement patterns. When movement and academics are integrated with ease and fluency, learning will be easier and less stressful.

One final note, children have a tendency to hold their breath when attempting movement that is difficult, so remind them to BREATHE! In some holistic programs, breathing is the essence of the program and brings about tremendous change by itself.

S'cool Moves for Learning

Chapter 3

The Small Group Design

"By kindergarten age, children should have learned the automatic movement adjustments necessary to maintain balance and posture and should no longer consciously attend to their movements. This frees them to concentrate on the perceptual information within the immediate learning environment– that is, school.

Margot Heiniger
The Integrated Motor Activities Screening

- What is Needed for Small Groups and Individualized Sessions?
- Incorporating Small Groups into the Daily Routine
- Individualized Programs
- Organizational Tips
- Completing the Program
- Certificate of Participation
- S'cool Moves for Learning Summary Chart of Movements

The Small Group Design

What is Needed for Small Groups and Individualized Sessions?

A quiet place is needed for the small group or the individualized program. Realizing there is limited space in most schools, it is important to secure a location for the program. Look at overall schedules and coordinate possible times to have a room for half hour blocks. Get creative and space will become available, even in the most crowded schools.

If teachers want to use the one-on-one model with the students in their classrooms only, then an assistant can work with children in the back of the classrooms. The novelty of certain children doing something different then the rest of the class wears off quickly.

Supplies and equipment needed:
one mat
10 carpet squares (13" wide x 17" long)
one rope (a regular clothesline rope works fine)
a variety of colored markers (children love the scented ones)
large sheets of white paper, 11" x 17" and 17" x 24"
newspapers
small plastic measuring scoops and dixie cups
two racket balls, soft balls of various sizes for catching activities

Optional equipment:
an easel or large marker board
Marsden Ball with bat
balance board

Incorporating Small Groups into the Daily Routine

Some schools have before school and after school programs for children needing extra academic help. Incorporating this program into their extended academic days works well. During the school day, small groups meet whenever it comfortably fits into the school schedule. Adding integrative movement to physical education classes is another way to fit the program into the school day.

A successful model for small groups is having one assistant work with two children at a time. To maintain quality instruction, a maximum of six students are paired with three assistants. The children rotate through three stations every five to seven minutes, depending on the amount of time allocated to each session (usually twenty to thirty minutes).

If possible, turn off fluorescent lights and utilize dim, natural lighting. At the start of the session, all children do Cross Crawls and Figure 8's. The children review their movements which are found in the pocket chart for the day's session (see organization tips later in this chapter). This saves time and allows children to rotate stations quickly. Each assistant works at one of the stations to guide children through the activities. A full discussion of each movement is covered in the following chapters.

The first station is the area for movements done on mats. The children do Cocoons, Extensions, balance movements, Angel Taps, Robo-Pats, and other floor level movement.

The second station is the jumping area where students use carpet squares and an oval rope to complete jumping activities.

The third station is the auditory- and visual-motor and eye-hand coordination area. Make tables available for seat work such as Squiggles, Figure 8's, or vision tracking worksheets. If possible, an easel is helpful for children who need to do their visual-motor activities standing at arm's length from the easel. Have a supply of markers, pencils, newspaper, and large white paper available. Organize vision training supplies, such as small cups, tracking balls, and pencils with cute eraser tops.

After each small group or individual session, allow for integration time. One way to do this is to have the children do the Roly-Poly. The Roly-Poly signifies the end to the session and creates a sense of closure and transition back to classroom activities. The child curls up into a flexed position and rolls back and forth, then side to side. The arms are looped around the knees to keep the knees tight into the chest. The forehead is brought as close to the knees as possible. Repeat two to three times in each direction.

Invite parents to participate with their child in the small group or individualized program one or two days a week so they can follow through at home.

Encourage parents or guardians to do deep pressure stimulation and integrative movement, such as belly crawling and creeping, to facilitate more growth in a shorter period of time.

Individualized Programs

Individualized sessions are organized based on days of the week (see next page). On Mondays and Wednesdays, do floor level and gross motor movement. On Tuesdays and Thursdays, complete vision tracking and auditory-visual-motor activities.

Friday is a good day to work with children who have been absent, or used to meet with other assistants or parents to discuss student progress and revisit program goals.

Organizational Tips

The S'cool Moves for Learning Summary Chart of Movements, provided at the end of this chapter, organizes all movement activities in chapters 4 through 11 from the lowest developmental level through the academic level. To monitor students' progress, assign a chart to each child and highlight current movement activities. As the child completes each movement, allow her to put a sticker or star in the square. Markers that have fun stamps on the end of them work well.

Copy off several charts, preferable on sturdy card stock, and cut the drawings into small cards. Laminate each movement to make individual cards that are used in a pocket chart. The pocket chart holds a file card with each child's name and individual cards to show the activities completed each session. This saves a lot of time that would be spent figuring out what movements the child is doing. Children enjoy the independence of looking at the pocket chart to find their name and movement activities without relying on the teacher to get them started each session. Children change cards to the next movement as they master the current movement.

Completing the Program

When children complete the program or no longer attend the sessions, it is appropriate to give a certificate or small token to acknowledge their progress and hard work. The certificate provided in this chapter may be used, or an original designed, with the school name, logo, and other personalized detail.

An individualized program may be organized in the following way:

Monday and Wednesday
Cocoon, Butterfly Wings, Butterfly Legs, and Extensions
Angels Taps or Robo-Pats
Balance movements
Jumping activities
Roly-Poly

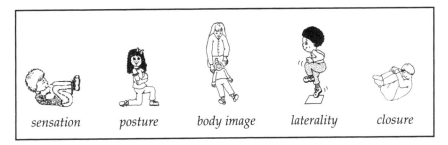

sensation   posture   body image   laterality   closure

Tuesday and Thursday
Figure 8's, auditory-visual-motor activities
Squiggles and Paper Crumpling
Vision tracking activities
Roly-Poly

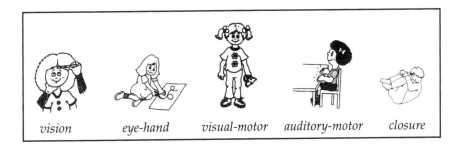

vision   eye-hand   visual-motor   auditory-motor   closure

Friday (optional day)
Time for self-evaluation: How am I progressing? What's easy? What's hard? What needs changing?

Certificate of Participation

S'cool Moves for Learning

Certificate of Participation

_____
Name

_____
Date

_____
Teacher or Assistant

You've Done
a Great Job!

S'cool Moves for Learning   *The Small Group Design*

S'cool Moves for Learning
Summary Chart of Movements

Name _____

Date _____

Sensation	Cocoon	Butterfly Wings / Butterfly Legs	Basic Extension / Butterfly Extension	Superman Extension
Posture	Low Level Balances	All Fours Balance	Pointing Balance	Knee Balance
Posture	Half-Kneel Balance	Sitting Balance	Sway Balance	One Leg Balance
Body Image	Angel Taps	Self-Portrait	Body and Partner 8's	Motor Planning Puzzles
Laterality/ Directionality	Cross Crawl	Robo-Pats	Ball-Games	Figure 8's

43

S'cool Moves for Learning
Summary Chart of Movements

Laterality/ Directionality	Carpet Squares (home base)	 Rope Jumping	 Hopping	 Skipping
Pre-Academics	 Listening Ears	 Clap-Tap Game	 Vision Exercises	 Monocular Vision
Pre-Academics	 Binocular Vision	 One Minute Vision Tracking	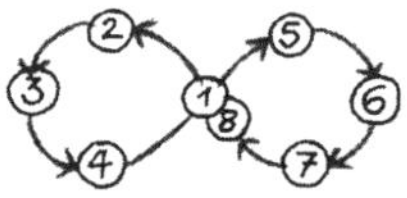 Figure 8's	 Snap Fingers
Pre-Academics	 Squiggles	 Paper Crumpling	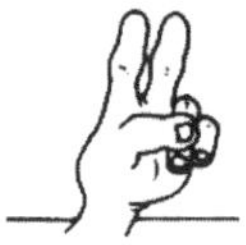 Rabbits	 Ok's
Pre-Academics/ Academics	 Sit and Pats	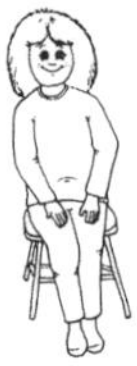 Palm Reversals	 Tossing and Catching	 One Minute Warm-Up for Writing

S'cool Moves for Learning

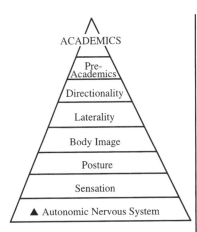

"If your body is like a car engine, sometimes you may feel like your engine is running in high speed, in low speed, or 'just right.' When your engine is in high speed, you may find it difficult to pay attention, to sit quietly in your seat, or get your work completed. When your engine is in low speed, you also may find it hard to concentrate, you may 'daydream' easily, or feel like a 'couch potato.' When you are in the 'just right' place, it's usually easier to pay attention, to get work done, and to have fun."

Mary Sue Williams and Sherry Shellenberger
How Does Your Engine Run?: A Leader's Guide to the Alert Program for Self Regulation

Chapter 4

Autonomic Nervous System (ANS)–Survival Systems: Setting the Foundation for Learning

- Chart of Behavior Review: ANS–Survival
- Student Profile: ANS–Survival
- Strategies for Success: ANS–Survival Level
- Movements for the Teacher and Students
  Morning Moves in Minutes: Starting the Day Energized, Focused, and Ready to Learn
  Munchies: Food for the Brain
  Mind: Water and Deep Breathing
  Music: Rhythm Tapping
  Motion: Cross Crawls and Figure 8's
  Listening Ears
  Sit and Pats

Chart of Behavior Review: ANS–Survival

❏ aggressive: physical and verbal
❏ arms disappear in clothing
❏ bizarre verbal outbursts
❏ cannot sit still
❏ clothes-sucking and shirt-turning
❏ constantly going to the bathroom
❏ does not finish work
❏ easily distracted
❏ everything is boring
❏ hyperactivity
❏ inappropriate self-touching
❏ itchy eyes
❏ knee-sitters and chair-rockers
❏ lacks eye contact
❏ off-task
❏ pencil chewing
❏ perfectionist or non-risk taker
❏ spaced-out
❏ speech difficulties
❏ stressful reading
❏ tears
❏ tension and stress from home or school
❏ trouble with boundaries

This page may be reproduced and used to monitor behavior of individual students.

Student Profile: ANS –Survival Level

Mary is a child who comes from a stressful home environment There are many children in her family, and much fighting among family members. When Mary gets to school, she appears tense and serious. She is a quiet child and reserved with her emotions. She does not have many friends and socializing is difficult for her. Mary is very sensitive to loud noises and overreacts to noise in the classroom. She displays a general disorganization with items at her desk, and with her body when she attempts fine and gross motor tasks. Mary lacks the sense of wonder and lightness of being that is associated with young children. We would recommend to Mary's teacher that he use the Strategies for Success listed on the next page and the Morning Moves in Minutes presented in this chapter to reduce her stress level.

Josh is also experiencing difficulty with his ANS and is "checked-out" and unmotivated. Josh needs help becoming more alert and focused. Some ideas are given in the Strategies for Success section found on the next page. The Morning Moves in Minutes would help Josh become energized, focused, and ready to learn.

In addition, Mary and Josh would benefit from being involved in a small group or individualized S'cool Moves for Learning program as discussed in chapters 2 and 3.

The Morning Moves in Minutes work with both systems of the ANS, the sympathetic and parasympathetic. The sympathetic system ensures survival by preparing for movement and providing a quick response to danger, fear, or threat. The parasympathetic system is the peacekeeper, helping to regain balance after being threatened or stressed. The movement in this chapter integrate the ANS to function in a complimentary manner with neither system taking over. The systems are balanced and respond appropriately to the daily classroom stimuli.

Strategies for Success: ANS–Survival Systems

✓ Children exhibiting signs of stress in the sympathetic system need a calm environment: soothing voices, soothing music, soft lighting, warm room, deep pressure stimulation (chapter 5), and the appropriate movements outlined in this chapter.

✓ Children exhibiting signs of stress in the parasympathetic system need to have things in their environment that stimulate them: brisk massage, vibrant lighting, sour or crunchy food, hands-on activities, upbeat music, and the movements outlined in this chapter that increase alertness levels.

✓ Read *How Does Your Engine Run?: A Leader's Guide to the Alert Program for Self Regulation* by Mary Sue Williams and Sherry Shellenberger (1996) for a complete discussion on alertness levels and how to teach children self-monitoring techniques. Providing children with appropriate strategies to change alertness levels transfers the responsibility from the teacher to the child.

✓ Children with focus difficulties do not have the internal time clock that other children naturally have. They must get feedback externally. Letting children know how long they are expected to focus may help. Setting a timer for a certain amount of time provides a clear expectation. Taping an index card on the desk and stamping the card with stars and other fun pictures when children are tuned-in helps maintain focus. Gradually reduce the amount of external reinforcement needed as children develop their internal time clocks.

✓ Encourage children to drink water at school. This keeps the brain hydrated and ready to learn.

✓ Orderly classrooms create a sense of safety and security. Post rules in a place where everyone can see them and be sure they are consistently and fairly followed.

✓ Scheduled daily routines help students organize their world.

✓ Children appreciate personal space. Allow those who need more space to have their desks away from other students.

- ✓ Decrease learning stress by using personal connections, prior knowledge, role play, mind maps, and overviews to introduce new subject areas. These activities activate the brain and readies it for learning.

- ✓ A child's age may be a guide for approximate focus time before needing a break. For instance, if a child is six, his average attention span will be about six to ten minutes.

- ✓ The peak time for learning detailed information such as spelling, rote learning, problem-solving, test review, report writing, math, and science is from 9:00 a.m. to 12:00 p.m. Movement-oriented tasks, paperwork, manipulatives, computer work, music, singing, and art is best from 12:00 p.m. to 2:00 p.m. The time from 2:00 to 5:00 p.m. is good for studying and physical activities.[1]

- ✓ Build on what children know, keep challenges to a point where they can accomplish the next steps and be successful.

- ✓ Students stay motivated to learn when they have control over their learning environment through choice, expression of ideas, and the freedom to create.

- ✓ Provide a learning environment that honors unique learning styles. Present information to appeal to auditory, visual, and kinesthetic learners.

- ✓ Give children the option to work independently, with a partner, or in small cooperative groups.

- ✓ Music can be calming or stimulating offering one of the best ways to change the mood of a group. When chosen carefully, music can help bring children to that "just right" place where they are not too energized or too mellow.

- ✓ If the classroom is filled with variety, novelty, and fun, as well as being emotionally stimulating and safe for risk-taking, then the ANS will function optimally and learning will be phenomenal!

Movements for the Teacher and Students

Morning Moves in Minutes: Starting the Day Energized, Focused, and Ready to Learn

Munchies: Food for the Brain
Eat Well
Children need fat and protein for the myelinated nerve fibers in the brain to create fast and efficient processing. Adding fruit such as bananas or oranges rounds out a great breakfast or snack for children.

Mind: Water and Deep Breathing
Drink Water
Encourage children to start their day with water. Water reduces mental fatigue and improves concentration. It is important for students to stay hydrated throughout the day.

Breathe Deeply
During deep breathing, the inhale breath causes the abdomen area to expand, rather than the chest. The exhale breath is through the mouth. Deep breathing can be done any time during the day to refresh or calm the mind and body.

Sometimes a child needs to experience deep breathing in an explicit way to understand how to breathe correctly. Have the child lie down and place a light weight book on his belly. As he breathes in, explain that the book goes up with the deep inhalation breath. The book goes down on the exhale.

Music: Rhythm Tapping
While playing music with a beat of 60–80 beats per minute, have the children tap their bodies with their palms or fingertips to the beat of the music (see reference section for music suggestions). Begin tapping the thighs and move down the leg to the ankles and feet. Move back up the body to the hips and shoulders. Tap the head. Tap all around the eyes, cheeks, and chin. Tap and rub the all around the outside of the ear and earlobes. Most children love rhythm tapping and it allows them the sensation of touch that many children miss at home or school. This movement increases alertness levels in children. [2]

Motion: Cross Crawls and Figure 8's

<u>Cross Crawls</u>
While standing, the children and teacher slowly touch their right hand or elbow to their left knee, then the left elbow to the right knee. Repeat Cross Crawls for a minute or more. Do Cross Crawls slowly for optimal body-mind integration. During Cross Crawls, large areas of both brain hemispheres are activated simultaneously. When this movement is done regularly, more nerve networks form between the brain's hemispheres, making communication between the two hemispheres faster and more efficient. Cross Crawls improve balance, gross motor, and fine motor skills. For a full discussion, including modifications, refer to chapter 8.

<u>Figure 8's</u>
An easy, quick way to switch on the visual system, improve laterality and directionality, and activate whole-brain thinking is to have children do Figure 8's either in the air or on 11 x 14 paper. The Figure 8 is drawn horizontal. Begin making the horizontal 8 by going up the middle and making a circle around to the left. Go back up the middle again and make a circle to the right. Repeat the movement several times, slowly. Use one hand, the other hand, and both hands clasped together. For a full discussion of the many variations and modifications, refer to chapter 8.

Listening Ears

With the thumb and index fingers, pull, uncurl, and massage the ear lobes, starting at the top of the lobe and ending with the bottom of the lobe. This activity helps focus attention on hearing and relaxes tension in the cranial bones for clearer focus. The child's ability to tune-in to relevant information improves. These are great to do before spelling tests.[3] Adding Cross Crawls after Listening Ears improves integration.

Sit and Pats

While sitting in a chair with their hands on their laps, children pat out the alphabet, number facts, or spelling words while keeping a beat of two pats per side. As children get better at this, the beat can change to two pats on one side and one pat on the other side. Sing, chant, or rhyme during Sit and Pats.

Use integrative movement whenever it is needed so children are at that "just right" place where learning is easy and fun.

S'cool Moves for Learning

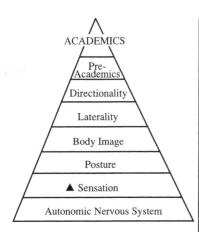

"No one part of the central nervous system works alone. Messages must go back and forth from one part to another, so that touch can aid vision, vision can aid balance, balance can aid body awareness, body awareness can aid movement, movement can aid learning, and so forth."

Carol Stock Kranowitz
The Out-of-Sync Child

Chapter 5

Sensation: Processing Information Through all the Senses

- Chart of Behavior Review: Sensation
- Student Profile: Sensation
- Strategies for Success: Sensation
- Integrative Movement and Activities
  Deep Pressure Stimulation
  Cocoon
  Butterfly Wings
  Butterfly Legs
  Basic Extension
  Butterfly Extension
  Superman Extension
  Extension Trio
  The Developmental Symphony I

Chart of Behavior Review: Sensation

- aggressive: physical and verbal
- arms disappear in clothing
- awkward pencil grip
- bizarre verbal outbursts
- cannot sit still
- clothes-sucking and shirt-turning
- clumsiness
- covers one eye; work placed to one side
- easily distracted
- everything is boring
- face on top of paper
- humming noises
- hyperactivity
- inappropriate self-touching
- itchy eyes
- knee-sitters and chair-rockers
- lacks eye contact
- no paper hold while writing
- off-task
- pencil chewing
- perfectionist or non-risk taker
- spaced-out
- speech difficulties
- stressful reading
- tears
- tongue helps out during tasks
- trouble with boundaries
- writing very light or dark
- writing very small, large, uphill, downhill

This page may be reproduced and used to monitor behavior of individual students.

Student Profile: Sensation

Kevin is repeating kindergarten and not having much success his second time around. He is in and out of his seat constantly, dropping things, and breaking crayons and pencils. He pulls Mary's hair, makes humming noises, talks aloud inappropriately, and doesn't listen well. Kevin does not like to be touched and is defensive when the teacher accidentally puts her hand on his shoulder. He frequently shoves the other children when lining up, and causes fights on the playground. Kevin is experiencing difficulty processing information through the sensory systems of the body.

Kevin would benefit from beginning his day with Morning Moves in Minutes as described in the previous chapter. The movements in this chapter would strengthen his posture and improve his ability to process information through the visual, auditory, tactile, and kinesthetic systems. The movements are based on the earliest movement patterns observed in infants. The Cocoon is derived from neonatal flexion that occurs in the womb. Butterfly Wings and Butterfly Legs mimic the movement of infants as they rub their body parts together to "switch on" the sensory system. The Extensions are based on infant's early movement patterns as they extend their bodies in preparation for more complex movement such as rolling over, sitting, belly crawling, and creeping on hands and knees.

The Strategies for Success provide ideas to help students like Kevin function in the classroom. Some ideas for how parents can involve their children in movement activities at home are included in this section, as well.

Strategies for Success: Sensation

✓ Children experiencing difficulties with sensation may have a variety of challenges in the classroom. They may be sensitive to touch, lighting, visual, and auditory stimuli. The best help for these types of children can be found in literature related to sensory integration difficulties.

✓ Children with fatigue posture, usually associated with sensation difficulties, may find sitting on the floor more comfortable than sitting in a chair. The floor is very grounding for some children and reduces the amount of effort required to work against gravity.

✓ Children with sensation difficulties become very wiggly and squirmy when focusing on seat-work. It is helpful for the teacher to apply a few seconds of firm pressure to the child's shoulders to help center and focus him. Always ask for permission from the parents and child before doing the shoulder pressure. Children can apply their own pressure while sitting in their chairs by pushing the palms of their hand together, squeezing the forearms and shoulders, pushing on the tops of the tables with their hands, and pressing on the tops of their thighs as if to push the feet into the floor. This creates sensory feedback and joint awakening for the body.

✓ Refer interested parents to *Kids Learn From the Inside Out* (see references) or to a knowledgeable physical or occupational therapist to learn how to do deep pressure stimulation with the child at home. Some children with sensory integration difficulties will not be comfortable with deep pressure, initially. Deep pressure stimulation helps children perform the movements described in this chapter by providing them with increased information about body position from muscles, joints, and ligaments. Have parents hold their child in the cocoon position when the child is in a lap-sitting or snuggling mood to help improve sensation.

Integrative Movements and Activities

Review Rhythm Tapping to assist with "switching on" sensation (chapter 4).

Deep Pressure Stimulation

Deep pressure stimulation helps the child get the sense of where his body is in space, and improves his ability to take in information from the environment. The child can do his own deep pressure stimulation by applying pressure to each hand, with the thumb of one hand pressing into the opposite palm. The child can squeeze his own forearms, upper arms, and shoulders, as if to give himself a hug. He can press his thighs firmly with his hands and try to press his feet into the ground.

Cocoon

<u>Movement Description</u>
While lying on the back with arms folded across the body and palms lightly touching shoulders, the child bends both knees while keeping the feet flat on the floor. On command, he "curls" the entire body in one movement—the upper body leading with the head, the chest, and the lower body, while bringing the knees to the chest and the ankles up at the same time. This should be done automatically and rapidly as a total unit. This position should be held for 3 to 5 seconds initially. Increase holding time from 30 to 60 seconds. The eyes should be looking down.

<u>Movement Progression</u>
This action is frequently simplified. Begin with the child's head resting on a pillow, arms crossed and feet against the wall with knees bent. On command, "curl" from this position. Curl the head and chest while bringing the knees away from the wall into the chest. The knees are held together with the ankles up. Increase the amount of time in this position and eventually do the Cocoon as described above.

To transition from the simplified movement to an independent Cocoon, the assistant may offer support to the child's head and legs while the child curls into the Cocoon. Another way to simplify this movement is to have the child do the Cocoon while lying on his side. This can usually be done by most children.

Compensating Behavior
A child may perform this action in segments or very slowly. The correct performance is to do it rapidly with the top and bottom of the body working simultaneously as the body curls into the Cocoon. There may be a head lag, as if the head is too heavy. There may be facial grimacing as a compensation to contracting the neck muscles. The child may be unable to maintain the arm position, but catch his arms either under his knees or below his knees. The bending of the knees to the chest should be done with the action of the hips. Frequently the knees will not be held together and the toes will be pointed. The child may roll over onto one side or the other and be unable to hold the position on his back. The curl may not be nice and tight. Instead the child may figure out how to hold the position by keeping distance between his head and knees. Encourage the child to curl as tight as possible.

Butterfly Wings

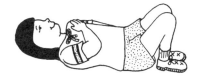

Movement Description
While lying on the back, the child begins with her arms down by her side. This movement has six fluid parts that blend into one another. One arm rubs across the torso in three ways: from one side of the body to the opposite shoulder (1) and back to the starting side (2) rub across the stomach to the opposite side (3) and back to the starting side (4) rub across the lower abdomen to the hip (5) and back to the starting side (6). Do the same pattern with the other arm. The palm and arm stay in contact with the body through all six movements.

Compensating Behavior
The child may do these movements fast. Movement will not be in a smooth controlled manner, but consist of jerky short movement. The forearm and elbow will not make continual contact with the chest. The arms need to be in constant contact during the entire movement.

Butterfly Legs

Movement Description
While lying on the back, the child's starting position is knees bent and feet flat on the floor. The child bends her knees into the chest and rubs her legs together allowing as much of the inner border of the legs to touch as possible, especially knees and ankles.

The movement should be long with one leg straightening as the other leg bends. Repeat three to five times. If possible, do this movement with the shoes off to get better contact and kinesthetic feedback. This movement may work better in the home environment than at school.

Simplify this action if a child is unable to bend his hips and keep his knees bent and against each other because of stomach or hip weakness. To simplify, begin with the child's knees bent and feet flat against the wall. This modifies the movement so that the child does not have to work against the force of gravity and has more success holding the knees together, keeping the inner borders of the legs touching. It will not be possible to fully straighten one leg while bending the other. Repeat three to five times. If possible, do this movement with shoes off to get better contact and kinesthetic feedback.

Compensating Behavior
The child may be unable to assume the starting position with flexed hips and knees and have difficulty keeping the hips together while doing the movement. The child may move fast or in an uncontrolled manner. The child may be unable to bend one leg while extending the other, or be unable to keep the legs touching.

Movement Progression
After arm and leg movement are done individually, they can be done at the same time. This is a very high-level integration of the top and bottom of the body. Most children will have difficulty doing these movement patterns together, although it's worth a try and provides a challenge for those who are ready.

Basic Extension
Movement Description
While the child is lying on his stomach with his arms and legs extended, he lifts his upper chest and tucks his chin on command while maintaining extension of his arms and legs. The child holds this position for 5–10 seconds progressing to 30–60 seconds. Have the child roll over on his side and get up from a side sitting position to enhance balance and ease the back. The eyes should be looking down.

Movement Progression
The child may need to lift just the trunk at first, and then the legs, separately.

Compensating Behavior
The child may only be able to lift his head up without tucking it into the chest or only momentarily lift his head and chest up with the elbows are bent and the arms off the floor. The child may be unable to lift his legs without bending his knees.

Butterfly Extension
Movement Description
While lying on the stomach, the child bends his arms and brings his elbows next to the chest. His palms are flat and level with his shoulders. On command, the child lifts and tucks his chin while raising his upper chest, arms, and legs. The elbows should be tucked next to the body. Hold this position for 5–10 seconds and progress to 30–60 seconds. Have the child roll over on his side and get up from a side sitting position to enhance balance and ease on the back. The eyes should be looking down.

Movement Progression
If the child is having difficulty keeping his elbows tucked in, have him return to a sitting position and touch his arms to his shoulders. Teach him how to rotate his shoulders with the elbows tucked down and in toward the body. The back should not arch.

Compensating Behavior
The child may be unable to lift and tuck his chin in one movement. Instead he will lift up first, and then tuck the chin. He will have difficulty keeping elbows in this bent position near the body. He may be able to raise the body only momentarily, and have difficulty keeping the knees straight.

Superman Extension

Movement Description
While lying on the stomach, the child's arms are resting on the floor above her head, with palms facing down. On command, she lifts her head and looks upward, while raising her arms off the floor and extending her legs. Repeat for 3–5 sets. For children having difficulty raising their trunk, hold a ball out in front of them and have them tap on it. Keep moving the ball a little higher to encourage lifting the

trunk. Have the child roll over on her side and get up from a side sitting position to enhance balance and ease the back.

Compensating Behavior
The child may be unable to lift her arms with the elbows extended, or be unable to hold the position.

Movement Progression
When doing extensions, it is best to learn the three extension patterns separately. During the Superman Extension, have the child hold the position and rock the body like a boat or rocking horse. After each pattern is completed successfully, put the three patterns together, doing them in sequence (Basic Extension, Butterfly Extension, and Superman Extension).

Extension Trio
Movement Description
Have the child put the three extensions together in a pattern beginning with the Basic Extension, moving into the Butterfly Extension, and ending with the Superman Extension. Repeat the trio three times.

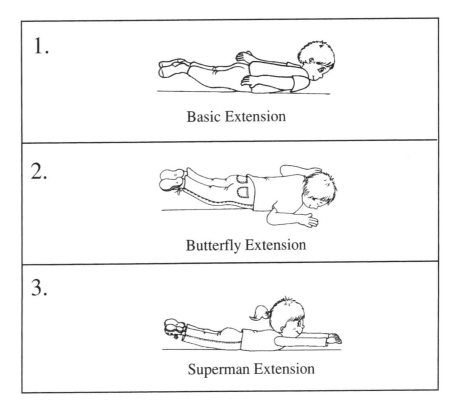

1. Basic Extension
2. Butterfly Extension
3. Superman Extension

1. Cocoon

2. Cocoon on the side

3. Basic Extension

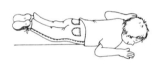

4. Butterfly Extension

5. Superman Extension

6. Cocoon on the side

7. Cocoon

The Developmental Symphony I

The Cocoon and Extensions are the early movement patterns that help develop the sensory system, strengthen the muscles needed for good posture while sitting at a desk, and reading and writing in an upright position. Gross and fine motor skills develop from this foundation. The Developmental Symphony I is a way for children to use their bodies to understand rhythm, pace, and sequencing—important elements of speech, language, reading, writing, and learning in general.

Movement Description

Begin in the Cocoon position and then roll over on the side while staying in the Cocoon position. From this position, roll over to the belly and flow into the Basic Extension. Complete the extension trio. End the Developmental Symphony by rolling back over to the side while curling into the Cocoon. Roll onto the back, staying in the Cocoon.

This is a fun way to put the Cocoon and Extensions together into a dance, of sorts. Playing soft, relaxing music, and focusing on breathing will help to integrate these movements.

1. Begin in the Cocoon position.
2. Roll onto the side in the Cocoon position.
3. From this position, roll over to the stomach and flow into the Basic Extension.
4. From the Basic Extension, move into the Butterfly Extension.
5. Next, move into the Superman Extension.
6. Roll to the opposite side of the one used in step 2, and move into a Cocoon on the side.
7. Roll onto the back, and end the sequence with the Cocoon.

Movement Sequence Summary

Cocoon ⇨ Roll to side ⇨ Cocoon on the side ⇨ Roll to belly ⇨ Basic Extension ⇨ Butterfly Extension ⇨ Superman Extension ⇨ Roll to the other side ⇨ Cocoon on the other side ⇨ Cocoon on the back

Movement Progression

Do the Developmental Symphony with eyes closed. Call out the directions of right and left.

S'cool Moves for Learning

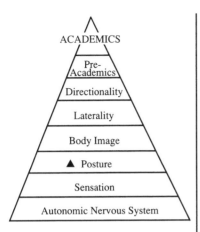

"Many children must depend upon body tension to maintain balance...Children with inadequately developed balance find it difficult to sit or stand quietly. They often have short attention spans and are most comfortable when in motion."

Elizabeth Davies
Perceptual-Motor Remedial Activities and Developmental P.E. Continuum

Chapter 6

Posture: Balance and Muscle Tone Needed for Academics

- Chart of Behavior Review: Posture
- Student Profile: Posture
- Strategies for Success: Posture
- Integrative Balance Movements
  Forearm Balance
  Rocking Balance
  All Fours Balance and Half-Kneel Balance
  Knee Balance
  Sitting Balance
  Standing Balance
  Sway Balance
  The Developmental Symphony II

Chart of Behavior Review: Posture

- ❏ aggressive: physical and verbal
- ❏ awkward pencil grip
- ❏ cannot sit still
- ❏ clothes-sucking and shirt-turning
- ❏ clumsiness
- ❏ doesn't finish work
- ❏ easily distracted
- ❏ falls out of chair
- ❏ humming noises
- ❏ hyperactivity
- ❏ inappropriate self-touching
- ❏ knee-sitters and chair-rockers
- ❏ lack of eye contact
- ❏ no paper hold while writing
- ❏ off-task
- ❏ pencil chewing
- ❏ perfectionist or non-risk taker
- ❏ sitting on edge of chair
- ❏ slow starter
- ❏ spaced-out
- ❏ speech difficulties
- ❏ stressful reading
- ❏ tongue helps out
- ❏ trouble with boundaries
- ❏ whole body lays on desk
- ❏ wraps legs around chair
- ❏ writing very light or dark
- ❏ writing very small, large, uphill, downhill

This page may be reproduced and used to monitor behavior of individual students.

Student Profile: Posture

Benjamin usually slouches, whether he is sitting or standing. When he is reminded to sit or stand up straight, he obeys for the moment but returns to his slouchy posture within minutes. He leans against anything he can find. Sometimes his mom feels like she has to literally hold him up to walk down the hall at school. Benjamin wiggles and squirms constantly in his seat, driving his teacher crazy. Benjamin has a difficult time with writing and academics, in general. He does not like recess or sports, and just hangs around while the other children play. Benjamin is showing signs of fatigue or weak posture, and it is affecting his ability to focus and complete his school work.

Benjamin would benefit from the movements in this chapter. Additionally, he may need some of the movements in chapter 5 if he is unable to do Cocoons or Extensions. If he is able to complete the movement activities in the sensation chapter, then we would assume his difficulties stem from poor balance.

The movement activities in this chapter are designed to improve kinesthetic feedback, balance, and muscle tone.

At the end of this chapter, the movements from the sensation chapter and this chapter are put together into the Developmental Symphony II. The pattern signifies the complex movement process infants develop from birth—flexing, extending, belly crawling, creeping, and standing. Children enjoy the challenge of learning and performing the Developmental Symphony!

Strategies for Success: Posture

✓ Provide activities out of seats and on the floor. Carpet squares help give students a sense of their own space. Children with balance difficulties may improve dramatically in their writing when allowed to write at floor level. Teachers will say, "But I can't have some children out of their seats while others sit at their desk." Here is an experiment: for one week let children sit wherever they want while doing their writing. Most children will return to their desks and find it awkward to do a lot of writing while sitting on the floor. Notice if writing improves while sitting on the floor for those children with balance problems. If so, encourage the children to write at floor level by giving them their own clipboard or hard writing surface.

✓ Encourage children with balance difficulties to use large markers and crayons at arms length, rather than small crayons and pencils. This will allow for visual-motor practice in a less physically demanding way.

✓ Give positive feedback when children use good posture during seat work and reading. The head should be straight and in line with the shoulders. The spine should be straight with the feet planted firmly on the ground, if the desk fits...which leads us to the next point.

✓ Have desks and chairs fit the child properly. The child's feet should touch the floor while sitting, and the desk or table should be a comfortable level for writing.

✓ Refer parents to the book *Kids Learn From the Inside Out* (see references) and encourage them to complete the belly crawling and creeping activities with their child at home. Generally, these activities are done with better success at home then in the typical school setting, as there is usually not enough space and time in the classroom to complete these movement patterns.

✓ Some programs recommend having children spin. Many children experience dizziness and discomfort. Use good judgement when choosing to spin or twirl.

✓ Physical Education classes can add lower-level movement whenever appropriate. Many programs start with children in a standing position. Create obstacle courses that have children crawl under and over items. Use directionality terms along with the movements.

✓ Backpacks are used frequently by students. Teach children the proper way to use their backpacks so they do not hurt their backs or develop poor posture. Backpacks should weigh no more than 5 to 10 percent of a child's body weight. A backpack with individualized compartments helps position contents more effectively. The child should wear both shoulder straps to keep weight evenly dispersed across the back. Straps should be padded so they do not dig into the child's shoulders. Shoulder straps need to be adjusted so the backpack fits the child's body.[1]

✓ Computer tables and chairs should be properly adjusted to fit the child. Children should sit erect with lower back supported and eyes level with the top of the screen. Encourage frequent stretch breaks. When setting up a computer lab or station, refer to ergonomic information for children to ensure postural requirements are met.[2]

Integrative Balance Movements

All balance movements should be done slowly. Some are done with the eyes open at first and then with the eyes closed. Closing the eyes develops an internal awareness of balance and kinesthesia since the visual system in not involved.

Resistive pressure is a technique that activates muscle action along the spine and strengthens the main muscle groups responsible for balance. Pressure is applied to the child's shoulders and hips while twisting the body in kneeling, sitting, and standing positions. The child resists being pushed off balance while his hips or shoulders are being pressed forward and backward causing the torso to twist. When applying resistive pressure, be sure to apply only in brief lengths of time. If the pressure is held too long, the child leans into it and does not use the core muscles to balance.

Review Cocoon and Extensions (chapter 5) to be sure the foundational work for balance is in place.

Forearm Balance

<u>Movement Description</u>

The Forearm Balance is a developmentally low balance. While on the stomach, have the child push up to her forearms and look around. She should hold this position for ten seconds without collapsing. The head should turn and look at the feet in both directions. The eyes need to look up and rotate around toward the feet in both directions. Most children in the regular classroom can balance at this level. Ask permission to touch the child before using resistive pressure in all the following balance movements.

<u>Movement Progression</u>
Provide resistive pressure to the child's side of the head, shoulders, and body in all directions. This should be done with the child's eyes open and then closed. Say, "Don't let me move your head" or "Don't be a pushover."

Ask the child to look around, up, down, and turn head to each side. Finally, have the child move the top of her body by walking on forearms from side to side. The work is done by the upper body. While on the stomach, the child pushes up to elbows and lifts one arm, pointing forward with the elbow straight.

While the child is on her stomach, she pushes up to her elbows and lifts one arm, up and out to the side. While on the stomach, push up to the elbows and draw Figure 8's in the air with the free arm.

Compensating Behavior
The three important factors to these movements are the ability to assume the position, hold the position for 10 seconds, and resist being pushed off balance with eyes open and then closed.

Rocking Balance

Movement Description
While the child is lying on her stomach, she pushes up to her elbows as in the forearm balance and moves from the elbow balance to pushing her upper body back over her hips as pictured in the drawing. Have the child stay in this position for 5–10 seconds. This movement is terrific for developing flexibility and actively stretching the back and hip area.

Movement Progression
The child can rock her hips back and forth, and walk hands in toward the body and out away from the body. To strengthen the upper body, have the child lift her arms while keeping her head down.

Compensating Behavior
Children with tightness in their back and hips will be unable to assume this flat back position and will have a rounded spine. They will be able to rock back and forth but will do it rapidly, rather than slowly. Their trunk muscles will be weak and unable to maintain a straight flat back while they are doing this movement. The movement should be continued, even with a rounded back to provide an active stretch to tight muscles. Also watch for elbows bending and shoulders sagging.

All Fours Balance

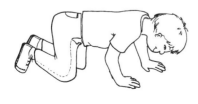

Movement Description
While the child is on all fours, with elbows slightly bent, apply pressure resistance to his shoulders and hips. Be sure to apply light, tapping pressure rather than a constant pressure. With eyes open, say, "Be strong and stable. Don't let me push you over." Repeat with eyes closed.

Movement Progression

With the child on all fours, with elbows slightly bent, have him sway from side to side, backward and forward. Next, have him turn his head to one side while catching a ball with the hand of the opposite side. Do this movement with both sides of the body. In this position, move opposite limbs forward and backward in a stationary creeping pattern. Turn the head to the opposite side of the arm that is moving.

On all fours, with elbows slightly bent, have the child lift and point one extremity, then the other. Have him turn his head the opposite way of his extended arm. Repeat by extending the leg back with the knee straight. This is done one at a time while maintaining correct body position. To increase the difficulty, have the child maintain the position for 10 seconds and perform the movement with his eyes closed.

On all fours, with elbows slightly bent, the child lifts one arm and one leg from opposite sides of his body, as if to point with the lifted hand and foot. This requires greater control and coordination between both the sides of the body, as well as the upper and lower parts of the body. The child moves his head in the opposite direction of the arm that is pointed.

Compensating Behavior for All Fours Balances

Watch for lack of correct body position, locked elbows, sagging trunk, and doing the movement too quickly. Watch that the supporting elbow is not locked. When the elbow is locked, it is supported by bone in the joint rather than active muscle action and is considered a splinter skill. This is a pattern commonly seen as a compensation for lack of muscle strength. For example, watch how people stand. Most people will lock their knees (hyperextend them) rather than use active muscle strength.

The child may be unable to assume the position without swaying or wobbling, or be unable to do the movements slowly, and alternate from a one-sided pattern (homolateral) to a two-sided pattern (cross pattern). Hesitating is a compensating behavior. The palms should be flat on the floor and the child should not use the fingertips. The child may lean into the pressure and not actually use core muscles for balance. The child may have a difficult time moving his head away from the limb that is moved.

Knee Balance and Half-Kneel Balance

Movement Description

Have the child assume a position on both knees. Give a twisting pressure against the child's shoulders, first one way and then the other. Say, "Can you hold this position if I try to twist your shoulders? Hold yourself straight ahead while I twist your shoulders." Have the child repeat this movement with the eyes open and then with the eyes closed. Resistance pressure may also be applied to the hips when doing the program at home (not recommended in the school setting unless approved by the parents). The resistive pressure calls on the core muscles of the front and back of the body and assists with developing coordination between the top and bottom of the body.

Movement Progression

The child assumes the Half-Kneel Balance position with one knee bent and her foot flat on the floor. Give a twisting pressure against the shoulders, first in one direction and then the other. Say, "Can you hold a straight ahead position even if I try to twist your body?" Repeat with the other knee bent and the foot flat on the floor.

Have the child alternate from one knee to the other knee. See if this can be done in a smooth manner without the foot sliding forward. The foot should end up flat on the floor after each knee change. For an added challenge, have the child close her eyes and cross her arms across her chest or place her hands on top of her head. No resistive pressure is applied for this movement—there is plenty of challenge without it!

Compensating Behavior for all Knee Balances

Inability to maintain a straight position while the twisting resistance is applied may indicate a lack of stability and strength in the trunk and hip muscles. There may be a lack of flow from one position to the other, or loss of balance going from one knee to the other. The child may be unable to maintain crossed arms or hands on top of the head while alternating knees.

Sitting Balance

Movement Description

Have the child sit on the edge of a chair or stool while maintaining good posture. The child should keep his balance while resistance is applied in a twisting motion first against one shoulder, then the other. Say, "See if you can keep your body straight while I twist your shoulders." Have the child do this with the eyes open and then closed. Try this with children who are experiencing writing difficulties in the classroom. It is a quick check to see if balance is affecting their ability to develop good writing posture.

Compensating Behavior
The child may need continual reminding to maintain good posture instead of maintaining it automatically. There may be an inability to maintain the position when resistance is applied in a twisting motion. The child may compensate by using the arms to balance, or may not compensate at all and fall out of the chair during desk work, or avoid falling from the chair by wrapping his legs around the legs of the chair.

Standing Balance

Movement Description
Have the child assume a standing position with a good base of support (feet should be 3–6 inches apart) and knees slightly bent, rather than locked. Maintain the position with eyes open and eyes closed.

Movement Progression
Apply resistance to the child's shoulders in a twisting motion. Say, "See if you can keep your body straight while I attempt to twist your shoulders."

Compensating Behavior
The body may rock or the child may hyperextend the knees.

Sway Balance

Movement Description
While the child is standing with one foot in front of the other, she rocks her body forward and backward. Have the child do this movement with the eyes open and then with the eyes closed. For added challenge, the child can make circular motions with the arms while rocking.

Movement Progression
Have the child balance on one foot with her hands on her head. Switch legs and balance on the other foot. Balance with eyes open

and then with eyes closed. If the child has difficulty balancing on one foot, have the child hold onto a chair for support. Have the child practice balancing while holding onto the chair. Next, offer the child support by allowing her to hold onto your hand. After the child can balance easily with her arms down at her side or straight out to the side, add the hands on top of the head. If the child continues to have difficulty balancing on one foot, review the previous balance movements to be sure she can do them easily. Balancing on one foot is the foundation for jumping and skipping activities.

Progress to jumping activities (see chapter 8), hopping on one foot then the other, and finally skipping. The skipping sequence is taught in the laterality section.

<u>Compensating Behavior</u>
The child may have difficulty keeping one foot placed in front of the other. The body may sway and wobble in this position. She may have difficulty with eyes closed.

While balancing on one foot, the child may want to wrap a leg around the leg she is standing on. She may move around trying to maintain her balance. The tongue may stick out or the face may tense.

The Developmental Symphony II
The Developmental Symphony II is a series of movements blended together. The individual movements learned in the sensation and posture chapters are organized into a fluid movement pattern. These movements include Cocoon, Superman Extension, Rocking Balance, All Fours Balance, and Kneeling Balance. The Developmental Symphony is designed to help children improve their classroom skills including the ability to focus, follow directions, understand spacial concepts, develop laterality, and express directionality. The progression of movements bring together the earliest infant developmental patterns in a manner that encourages rhythm and flow from one movement into the next. These movements are an excellent way to actively stretch and strengthen muscles, improve body orientation in space, balance, and coordination. Children enjoy learning and performing the sequence to music.

S'cool Moves for Learning Posture

1. Cocoon

2. Cocoon on the side

3. Superman Extension

4. Rocking Balance

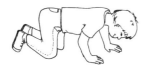
5. All Fours Balance

6. Kneeling Balance   7. Half-Kneel Balance

8. Standing

Movement Description
1. Begin in the Cocoon position.
2. Roll onto the side in the Cocoon position.
3. From this position, roll over to the stomach and flow into the Superman Extension.
4. From the Superman Extension, push back over the hips into the Rocking Balance.
5. Next, move through to the All Fours Balance.
6. From the All Fours Balance, move to the Kneeling Balance on both knees.
7. Next, move to the Half-Kneel Balance on one knee.
8. Finish in the standing position.

Repeat the sequence in reverse and finish with the Cocoon. When moving from standing to the floor level, be sure to have the child use the opposite knee and roll to the opposite side. For instance, if the child rolled to the right side and used his right knee at the start of the Symphony, he should use his left knee and roll to the left side to integrate both sides of the body. Emphasize breathing, smoothness, and relaxation while doing the movements.

Movement Sequence Summary
Cocoon ⇨ Roll to side ⇨ Cocoon on the side ⇨ Roll to belly ⇨ Superman Extension ⇨ Push back to Rocking Balance ⇨ Move to All Fours Balance ⇨ Kneeling Balance ⇨ Half-kneel ⇨ Standing

Reverse the sequence:
Standing ⇨ Half-kneel (other leg) ⇨ Kneeling Balance ⇨ All Fours Balance ⇨ Rocking Balance ⇨ Superman Extension ⇨ Roll to the other side ⇨ Cocoon on the side ⇨ Roll to back ⇨ Cocoon

Movement Progression
Do the movements with eyes closed. Call out the directions of right and left. For added challenge, after step 5, have the child balance with the opposite arm and leg out as shown in the picture on the right. Switch sides and balance with opposing arm and leg. Complete steps 6–8.

S'cool Moves for Learning

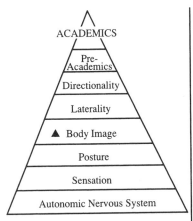

"A child who holds onto other children, runs a hand along the wall while walking, or frequently bumps into others may be demonstrating a lack of body awareness."

Margot Heiniger
The Integrated Motor Activities Screening

Chapter 7

Body Image: Staying Centered While the World Around Us Changes

- Chart of Behavior Review: Body Image
- Student Profile: Body Image
- Strategies for Success: Body Image
- Integrative Movements and Activities
  Angel Taps
  Self-Portrait Drawing
  Body 8's
  Partner 8's
  General Activities
  Motor Planning Puzzles

Chart of Behavior Review: Body Image

- ❏ aggressive: physical and verbal
- ❏ cannot sit still
- ❏ clumsiness
- ❏ hyperactivity
- ❏ knee-sitters and chair-rockers
- ❏ lack of eye contact
- ❏ writing from bottom-up
- ❏ writing very small, large, uphill, downhill
- ❏ writes with no space between words

Others
- ❏ clingy or whiny
- ❏ poor self-concept
- ❏ cries easily
- ❏ appears emotionally young
- ❏ poor spatial awareness
- ❏ hangs onto other children
- ❏ frequently in other children's personal space
- ❏ distracted by excess noise and visual stimulus

This page may be reproduced and used to monitor behavior of individual students.

Student Profile: Body Image

June is seven years old and is insecure and awkward around other children. Her writing is very small. When asked to draw a picture of herself, she draws a small stick figure with few details. She constantly needs to go to the bathroom, a form of escape she uses when things get tough. She loses her things and cannot find her "cubby." She cries because other children pick on her, take her things, and do not give her a turn at games. June likes to sit close to the teacher during story time and frequently wants to sit on her lap. June is clingy and unhappy most the time. She is having difficulty with her body image and needs opportunities to become more independent and self-confident.

The movements in this chapter would help June improve her body image, assuming she can do the movements in the sensation and posture chapters.

The body image movement activities help children develop an internal awareness of their body position in space, building the foundation for laterality and directionality to develop. Children with a good body image stay centered when the world around them is in constant flux. They "go with the flow" and transition easily from one classroom activity to another.

Chapter 12, our concluding chapter, features a young girl who started a movement program with poor body image. We have included her beginning self-portrait and her self-portrait after three months in the program. Her improvement in body image is apparent from one self-portrait to the other.

Strategies for Success: Body Image

✓ Children having difficulties with their orientation in space may also have difficulties seeing the components of a whole and breaking things into smaller parts. Examples include being unable to put lines together to form a shape, coordinate movement to perform a task, select syllables to make words, identify steps to directions, or put the pieces together for academics. Using whole body movement to learn concepts, numbers, and letters will help.

✓ Rhythm, pace, and sequencing are elements that give flow to movement and actions. These elements may be off in children experiencing body image difficulty causing them to be clumsy, trip over other children, and bump into objects around the room. They may irritate their classmates by not allowing appropriate space between themselves and others, leading to a constant invasion of their neighbor's space.

✓ Provide children with strategies to help them maintain their own personal space. For example, use carpet squares when children are sitting on the floor to make it easier for them to stay within appropriate boundaries. Offering the choice to move away from other children if they want to have more space for themselves may help with focus, and actually be less stressful for children with body image difficulties.

✓ Children with body image difficulties may have difficulties with auditory and visual figure-ground. Figure-ground is the ability to filter out what you do not want to see or hear, and tune in to what is important at the time. These children need limited visual stimulation. Reduce wall hangings, pictures, and decorations on bulletin boards. The flicker and buzz of fluorescent lights may also bother them. Turn off fluorescent lights when possible or use full-spectrum lighting.

Integrative Movements and Activities

Rhythm Tapping and Deep Pressure Stimulation are good to do before Angel Taps to improve sensation.

Angel Taps

Movement Description
With the child lying on her back with eyes closed, the assistant taps each limb, one at a time. The child slides the limb outward, and then slides the limb back to the body, as if creating a snow angel. Always end each movement with the child finding a "home" position. The home position is with the arms beside the body and legs closed and touching one another. Start in home position between each tap.

Movement Progression
Begin with each limb moving separately. After this is easily accomplished, begin tapping on two limbs on one side (arm and leg) and then tap on two opposite limbs (arm on one side of the body and leg on the other side of the body). Next, have the child moved her limbs by herself in a rhythmic manner. Do the following movements several times each: 1. Begin moving just the arms, out and in. 2. Move the legs out and in. 3. Move the arms and legs out and in together, making sure the upper and lower body limbs move at the same time. 4. Move the arm and leg on the right side of the body out and in. 5. Move the arm and leg on the left side of the body out and in. 6. Move the right arm and left leg out and in. 7. Move the left arm and right leg out and in. The movement should be done to different tempos, fluctuating from quick to slow. The patterns may be put together for smooth transition from one to another. Repeat the series of movements while on the stomach. The child tires easily in this position so do it for a brief amount of time. A pillow under the stomach may make the movements easier to accomplish.

Compensating Behavior
If the child must look at her limbs prior to moving them, she is compensating for not knowing where her body is in space. Moving more limbs than just those tapped shows signs of overflow (the inability to move one part of the body without other parts also moving). Leaning the body or head toward or away from the side being tapped also is a display of laterality difficulties.

Self-Portrait Drawing

Activity Description

Draw a self-portrait at the beginning of the school year, or at the beginning of participation in the program.

Movement Progression

Have the child draw a self-portrait periodically throughout the school year and during involvement in the program. It is quite fascinating to see the changes in the self-portrait as body image and self-awareness increases.

Compensating Behavior

The same compensations can be noted as when the child attempts to write. These include awkward pencil or crayon grip, head leaning, moving paper away from midline, small writing, not using the entire space on the paper, wrapping legs around chair for balance, or sitting to one side of the chair. The drawing may show lack of body image with an incomplete person, very small figure, or simple stick figure.

Body 8's

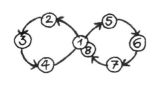

Movement Description

Have the child make the Figure 8 pattern (an 8 on it's side) with the nose, elbows, wrists, hips, and knees (while sitting). Let the child get creative and see what else she can come up with.

Partner 8's

Movement Description

Have children face each other in pairs and make 8's while their hands are touching, palm to palm or interlocking their fingers. The children work as partners to draw a Figure 8 together while facing each other and pressing on each other's hands. Be sure to emphasize starting the pattern up the midline and curving up and to the left. The facing partner will curve to the right. This movement is great for loosening the shoulder girdle for writing, crossing the midline of the body, and integrating the brain. Partners may also do 8's with their feet pressed together in a sitting position.

General Activities

Other activities that improve body image are those that have children actively involved with identifying and moving body parts. Have children play along with songs like Hokey-Pokey, Head-Shoulders-Knees and Toes, or Twister to improve body image.

Motor Planning Puzzles

Motor Planning Puzzles are also referred to as Balance Puzzles. They serve two purposes: motor planning and balance.

Activity Description

Cut figures out as described below. Paste the figures onto marker board or paper and laminate. Hold the puzzles up and have the child look at the puzzle and copy it with his own body.

Activity Progression

Initially, the child should be encouraged to place any corresponding hand and foot. Do not worry about the right and the left. As the child becomes comfortable with the process, add right and left directions.

Compensating Behavior

Do not worry about compensating behavior, just play and have fun!

Motor Planning Puzzle cutouts:

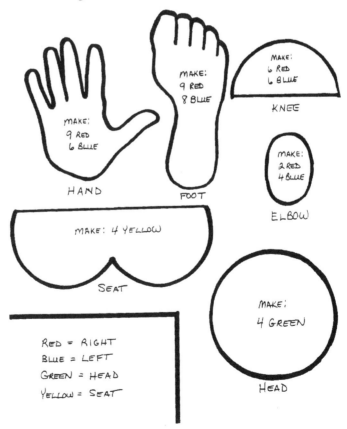

Below are examples of Motor Planning Puzzle arrangement. For very young children arrange the easiest patterns first (two feet, two knees, two elbows, one head, one bottom, etc.) and then move into these patterns.

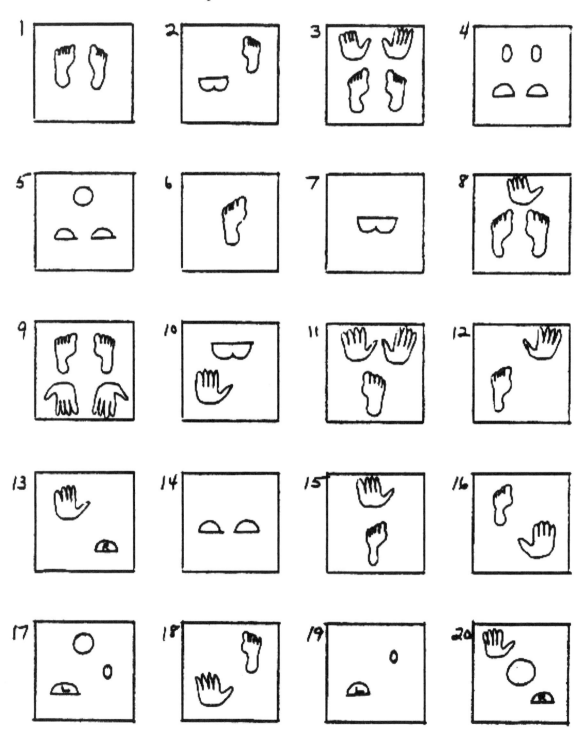

S'cool Moves for Learning

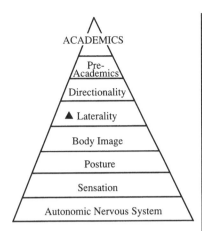

"Laterality must be learned. It is only by experimenting with the two sides of the body and their relationship to each other that we come to distinguish between the two systems...The primary pattern out of which this differentiation develops is that of balance. When experimenting with the balancing problem, the child must learn right and left, for he must learn how to innervate one side against the other, how to detect which side has to move, and how it has to move..."

Dr. Newell C. Kephart
The Slow Learner in the Classroom

Chapter 8

Laterality: The Internal Sense of Having Two Sides of the Body that Work Separately and Together

- Chart of Behavior Review: Laterality
- Student Profile: Laterality
- Strategies for Success: Laterality
- Integrative Movements and Activities
  Cross Crawls
  Robo-Pats
  Double Robo-Pats
  Cross Crawl Robo-Pats
  Ball-Games
  Figure 8's
  Carpet Squares I, II, III
  Jumping Activities
  Skipping Rope
  Hopping Activities
  Skipping

S'cool Moves for Learning   *Laterality*

Chart of Behavior Review: Laterality

- ❏ awkward pencil grip
- ❏ cannot sit still
- ❏ clumsiness
- ❏ covers one eye; work placed to one side
- ❏ difficulty forming letters and numbers
- ❏ face on top of paper
- ❏ hyperactivity
- ❏ knee-sitters and chair-rockers
- ❏ reversal of letters or numbers
- ❏ sitting on edge of chair
- ❏ stressful reading
- ❏ tongue helps out
- ❏ trouble with boundaries
- ❏ whole body lays on desk
- ❏ wraps legs around chair
- ❏ writing from bottom-up
- ❏ writing on one side of paper
- ❏ writing very small, large, uphill, downhill
- ❏ writes with no space between words

This page may be reproduced and used to monitor behavior of individual students.

Student Profile: Laterality

Maggie sits at her desk to write with her legs wrapped around the chair and her head lying down on the desk. Her work is placed to one side of the desk, and she uses just one side of the paper when writing. Maggie has difficulty forming letters and numbers and frequently reverses them. She forgets to hold her paper when she writes. Frequently, her tongue moves right along with her pencil or scissors. Hopping and skipping are difficult for her.

The laterality movement activities will help Maggie use one side or both sides of her body, together and separately. They will improve her ease of midline crossing and solidify the foundation for directionality to develop. Maggie should be able to do Cocoons, Extensions, and the balance and body image movements described in earlier chapters before being asked to do laterality movements.

Maggie's parents should be encouraged to play with her at home by making fun obstacle courses that involve crawling, creeping, and climbing.

Laterality helps children develop a dominant eye, hand, and foot. Processing between the right and left hemispheres of the brain becomes faster as children integrate laterality into the body-mind system. Children who are slow at processing information and get further behind each school year usually have difficulty with laterality.

Strategies for Success: Laterality

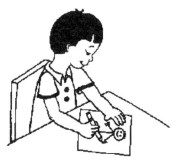

✓ Laterality difficulties affect children in many ways. All the Strategies for Success discussed in previous chapters may be applied to children having difficulty with laterality.

✓ Physical education classes should empathize gross motor movements that involve both sides of the body so children can naturally develop a preferred side. Do not try to force a child to use a particular side. This tends to frustrate the child and becomes counter-productive.

✓ Encourage children with midline difficulties to sit straight in their chairs and place their papers to the center of their desks and bodies. Watch out for compensating behavior such as leaning the head to one side or laying it on an arm. These children also tend to sit on one side of the chair to avoid crossing the midline while writing. Encourage all students in the class to use good posture for reading and writing activities.

✓ For a powerful classroom tool, read *The Dominance Factor: How Knowing Your Dominant Eye, Ear, Brain, Hand & Foot Can Improve Your Learning* by Carla Hannaford (1997). Dr. Hannaford's work in this area has proven to be an integral part of the S'cool Moves for Learning program. Teachers and students enjoy discovering their unique profiles and understanding how it influences their learning. Parents and children can grow in their understanding and appreciation for one another when they know their profiles.

✓ *Infinity Walk* by Deborah Sunbeck (1996) also has a chapter on understanding your brain's current sensorimotor patterns.

✓ The Figure 8 is an essential tool for developing laterality. When naming the sideways "8" discussed in this chapter and used throughout the program, a consensus could not be reached. "Race Tracks," "Crazy 8's," "Lazy 8's," "Figure 8's," and "Integr8ts" were approved by different classes. For the purpose of this book, the common name of Figure 8 will be used but it has a variety of names in various literature.

Integrative Movements and Activities

Review Angel Taps and prior movement patterns to be sure the foundation for laterality is in place.

Cross Crawls

Movement Description
While standing, slowly touch the right hand or elbow to the left knee, then the left elbow to the right knee. Repeat this motion for a minute or more. Do Cross Crawls slowly for optimal body-mind integration.

Movement Progression

Lying Down
For a child experiencing extreme balance and/or midline difficulties, the assistant may need to physically move the limbs through the Cross Crawl pattern while the child is lying down. Assist the child to progress from support to independence by having her move her arm and touch her hand to her opposing knee while the assistant moves just her knees. When the child first begins this movement without assistance, she may move both hands across the midline to one knee, and eventually learn to move one hand at a time across the midline. As the assistant moves the legs and the child moves her arms, reduce the amount of help given with the legs by providing a gentle tap to the opposing leg as the child begins moving the legs herself. This approach has worked for children as young as three years old.

Sitting
Once the child can do the movement on her own while lying down, progress to doing it in a sitting position. When first beginning the Cross Crawl pattern, the child may have more success if both hands touch each leg at the same time. Gradually, progress to the opposing hand and leg position. While sitting, it is easier to get more midline crossing by having the child touch her elbows to her opposite knee, rather than using her hands.

Standing
Performing Cross Crawls while standing is the highest level. The child may begin by using just one side of the body and then learn to use the opposing side. Quickly progress to the hand or elbow touching the opposing knee. For challenge and fun, play music

that has a slow beat and see how slowly the children can Cross Crawl. The slower the Cross Crawl is done, the more challenge to the vestibular system and the more integrating it will be. Children can add touching their opposite hands and feet to their toes and heels.

Compensating Behavior
While doing this movement standing, children with balance or midline difficulties will do it very fast. They will have very little hand movement, and compensate by keeping the hands very close to the center (midline) of the body. The arms stay almost crossed at the wrists and they tap their knees without needing to move their arms. There may be very little upper body movement. Children will keep their legs very wide apart to balance better.

Robo-Pats

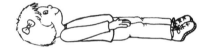

Movement Description
While lying on the back with arms at the side and legs together, the child lifts each arm and leg one at a time a few inches off the ground, progressing from the right arm, left arm, left leg, and right leg. After this is accomplished in a fluid pattern, have the child begin with a different arm or leg and proceed to lift in the same pattern (left arm, left leg, right leg, right arm).[1]

Movement Progression
After this movement can be done fluidly, do the movement while listening to someone talk, while carrying on a conversation, and while vision tracking to integrate the auditory and visual systems. This will minimize the risk of the movement becoming a splinter skill.

Compensating Behavior
The child's head or body may lean to the right or left, away from the midline. Pats may be very loud and clumsy. Reinforce quiet pats and smoothness between limb changes. The child may lift her limbs too high off the ground and need to be shown how high to lift each limb. Pats should be done rhythmically, without pauses between limb changes. Stopping in between limb changes is a sign that the child has to think too much and has not integrated the movement into the body-mind system. The child should be able to listen, talk, and track visually while doing the movement before progressing to a higher level Robo-Pat.

Double Robo-Pats

Movement Description

While lying on the back, with arms at the side and legs together, the child pats each arm and leg two times. The arms and legs should come a few inches off the ground, starting with the right arm, left arm, left leg, and right leg. After this is accomplished in a fluid pattern, begin with a different arm or leg and proceed to lift in the same pattern (left arm, left leg, right leg, right arm). The movement pattern is the same as single pats with the exception of patting each limb two times.

Movement progression and compensating behavior are the same as in single Robo-Pats. Robopats may be done while on the stomach.

Cross Crawl Robo-Pats

Movement Description

While lying on the back, in the same position as in former movements, the child pats her arm and leg on the opposite sides of the body two times. Alternate between the right arm/left leg, and left arm/right leg. Changes between the sides of the body should be smooth and fluid.

Movement progression and compensating behaviors are the same as in single Robo-Pats. Increase the difficulty by changing the pattern to two taps on one side and then one tap on the other side. Have the child say, "Tic-Toc" while doing this pattern. Fun!

Ball-Games

Movement Description

A group of children were doing these movements and started singing, "Take me out to the ball game." The name stuck. Ball-Games are done in three steps and put together rhythmically while moving from one step to the next.

Step I
While standing, the child does Cross Crawls.

Step II
While standing, the child extends her right arm overhead and left leg out to the side, in opposite directions. The child brings both

limbs back together. She switches sides and alternates sides so there is a flow and graceful change between the sides of the body. The child's feet come together on the floor between side changes.

Step III
While standing, the child takes a step backward. Stretch the same side of the body in opposite directions. The right leg will move backward and the right arm will move forward. Do this movement one time and switch sides. The left leg will move backward and the left arm will move forward. Keep alternating from side to side in a fluid motion. Feet come together on the floor between side changes.

Movement Progression
The child puts all three steps together by doing one complete set (one starting with the right side of the body, and one starting with the left side of the body). The child does one Cross Crawl as described in step I, flow into step II, and end with step III. There is no stopping between the steps. After this is accomplished with ease, increase effectiveness by having the child hum and roll eyes in large circles in both direction—a challenge for just about everyone, integrated or not!

Compensating Behavior
There may be stops between steps I, II, and III when attempting to put all three steps together. Children who stop are thinking about how to get the job done. If this occurs, practice each step separately before putting them all together. The movements may be done quickly to avoid balance or midline difficulties. The limbs may be bent instead of held straight. There may be tension observed in the body or face region.

Figure 8's

Figure 8's are versatile and effective at integrating both sides of the body, increasing the efficient midline crossing of the body, and directionality. Figure 8's have had various names in different programs. The Figure 8 is modified from Kephart's Lazy 8.[2]

Movement Progression
Walking 8's

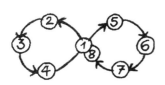

A Figure 8 pattern may be set up by placing two chairs in the center of the pattern and having the child walk the pattern around the chairs. The starting point for walking the pattern is between the two chairs. The pattern is walked as demonstrated in the drawing to the left. Begin with number 1 and walk the pattern as numbered. Have the child walk this pattern several times. When the child attempts to draw the pattern in the air or on paper, have her close her eyes and picture the chairs. This works wonderfully for young children.

Drawing 8's

Next, have the child practice drawing the Figure 8 on a desk. Drawing a Figure 8 on a desk provides a pattern for the child to trace with her hand when initially learning the movement. A permanent marker works fine and wears off after awhile. Also, children can trace an 8 on their desks whenever they need additional integration (before reading, math, etc.). A dab of shaving cream on the desk also works well. Drawing 8's in sand, on carpet squares, or on other tactilely interesting surfaces enhances the process. The 8 may be drawn on a large surface such as a marker board or easel. While sitting on the floor, draw Figure 8's on large sheets of paper. Finally, have the child draw a Figure 8 on large paper while sitting at her desk using a pattern to trace (kindergarten only). First grade children and older do not need to trace a pattern. Encourage good posture and proper pencil grip.

Use colored markers or crayons. Figure 8's may be done with the right hand, left hand, and then using both hands. When using both hands, usually the child places her dominant hand in its regular writing position and places the non-dominant hand above it. The child may perform the Figure 8's for a minute or so with each hand and with both hands. At the beginning of kindergarten, performing Figure 8's with only the dominant hand usually offers enough challenge. Add the non-dominant hand and both hands as the process becomes easier for the child. Encourage the child to perform the 8's slowly, with her eyes watching her marker. For added fun, let the child create a drawing at the end of the session, incorporating the 8 into the drawing.

Air 8's

Have the child draw the Figure 8 in the air while tracking her thumb with her eyes. Putting a sticker on the thumb may help provide a visual stimulus for tracking. The child aligns her body with a point at eye level. This will serve as the midpoint of the 8. The thumb is up and eyes are focused on the thumb nail. The thumb is at arms length. Either hand may be used first. Start at the midline and move counter-clockwise while drawing the 8. The thumb moves in an upward pattern while crossing the midpoint of the 8 (midpoint of the body). Including the entire visual field will bring the most benefit (up, down, and side to side). The eyes follow the 8, the head moves slightly, and the neck remains relaxed. Do three repetitions with the 8 in air while tracking the thumb. Do three repetitions using the other hand, then with both hands clasped together.

Balance 8's

While in the same position as described in Air 8's, have the child tilt her head to the right and pretend it is glued to the right shoulder. The child pictures the right hand as a paintbrush. The palm is down toward the ground and the fingers are straight out in front. While in this position the child bends the knees up and down while "painting" an 8 on the wall in front of the right arm. Paint many 8's and then switch sides and repeat the same movement with the left arm outstretched and the head glued to the left shoulder. This movement is great for stimulating the vestibular system. As with all 8 movements, be sure to have the child begin the 8 from the center of the body and move up to the right or left. Remember to go, "up the hill and around."

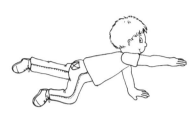

Pointer 8's
With the child on one knee with his opposite arm and leg extended, he draws a Figure 8 pattern in the air. Switch sides, using the other leg and opposite arm. This movement integrates sensation and posture. Have the child alternate from one arm and opposite leg to the other arm and opposite leg in a cross crawl fashion. Next have the child touch the opposite arm and leg together at the midline of the belly, bringing the knee and the hand in together. The hand touches the opposite knee. Alternate back and forth in a Cross Crawl manner. See if the child can maintain rhythm and flow with both movement patterns. Have the child listen and talk while doing the movement. Put the two patterns together—first with the opposite arm and leg away from the body, then with the opposite arm and leg touching inside by the stomach. With four counts, both patterns are completed.

Compensating Behavior for all Figure 8 Movements
Midline avoidance is observed when there are laterality difficulties. The head or body may lean away from the midline of the body. The Figure 8 may be uneven, showing preference to one side of the body or visual field. The paper may gradually move away from the midline of the body or the body may lean away from the writing area. When eyes are intentionally closed or look away while drawing the pattern, there may be eye-hand coordination difficulties. If the 8 improves while the child is not watching, suspect that the eyes and hands are not working together. Encourage the child to watch what the hands are doing. There is a tendency to do Figure 8's quickly. The Figure 8 integrates the body-mind system when it is done slowly, with flow and rhythm. If the Figure 8's are not improving midline difficulties, visual tracking, or general body-mind integration, observe the child while he is performing Figure 8's. Frequently the child is in a low state of body awareness. The child is in the "doing" state where the objective is merely to get them done. The child needs to be guided in slowing down, finding his midline, focusing his thinking on the 8 pattern, and really getting the sense of being in his body. Figure 8's are one of the most integrative movements available that can be done in minutes a day for dramatic change *when* they are performed correctly. For this reason we have dedicated quite a lengthy discussion on their behalf. Figure 8's can be done anywhere including in sand, with chalk on the sidewalk, or on a child's back. Look for every opportunity to use the great 8 to integrate!

Carpet Squares I
Activity Description
Begin with one carpet square designated as home base. Have the child jump forward, backward, and sideways while an assistant calls out the direction. After each direction is called, the child returns to home base for the next direction.

Activity Progression
Next, have the child call out herself what direction she is jumping, at the same time that she jumps. Use the instructions of forward, backward, and sideways. In doing so, there is a firm, total body commitment connecting the motor response with language.

Carpet Squares II
Activity Description
Use four carpet squares and designate one home base. Begin by having the child jump into a square as the assistant calls out a color. Once the child can jump smoothly, without hesitation, to commands that focus on carpet square color, begin using the commands of forward, backward, and sideways. As the child masters this activity, begin adding the directions of right and left.

Activity Progression
Next, have the child call out loud what direction she is jumping at the same time that she jumps. Use the instructions of forward, backward, sideways/diagonal, right, and left.

Carpet Squares III
Activity Description
With nine carpet squares, call out colors and directions for the child to jump as described in carpet square activities I and II. Turn the body in different directions so the child learns that positioning is in relationship to where the body is placed in space.

Activity Progression
Tape alphabet letters, spelling words, or numbers to a corner of the squares to add a kinesthetic element for learning these skills.

Compensating Behavior for all Carpet Squares Activities
The child may land with one foot ahead of the other, jump too fast, lose control, or hesitate while jumping with commands.

Jumping Activities

Activity Description

With the 25 foot rope laid on the floor in a rectangular shape, the child will jump using patterns 1–12 on the following pages. Have the child study the pattern first, then stop and focus before beginning. The starting position is at the base of the rope. The child should always keep her hands on her hips and look at the rope while jumping. The jumping should be smooth and controlled, not fast. The assistant can clap her hands rhythmically, or use a metronome. The jumping should not be heavy on heels or up on toes. [3]

Activity Progression

As each pattern is successfully completed, progress to a more difficult pattern. After all patterns are done easily, begin hopping on one foot using carpet square or rope patterns.

Compensating Behavior

The most usual compensation is for students to quickly rush through the patterns without controlled upper/lower body coordination. The faster these patterns are done, the easier it is to avoid problems with balance, midline crossing, and upper/lower body coordination. Momentum alone, propels the body forward. The eyes may look away from the rope if there is eye/foot coordination difficulties. The arms may be called into action to help out and not stay on the hips. The child may lean away from the midline of her body, thus managing to avoid the objective of the jumping activities. Observing this can be tricky. If the child's body leans away from where the feet land, midline crossing is reduced. The child may jump hard or up on the toes. The child may take long jumps to finish the activity quickly. He should be able to complete the entire pattern before he gets to the end of the rope.

Skipping Rope

Movement Progression

Begin by having the child jump over the rope with both feet while the rope is lying flat on the ground. Next, tie the rope to a table leg or have someone hold it, and gradually raise the rope while the child jumps over it. Next, add some movement to the rope so the child has to time his jumping. Progress to standing and jumping with both feet, and then opposite feet, while turning the rope.

S'cool Moves for Learning   *Laterality*

The footprints are for direction guidance only; this activity should be done while wearing good shoes.

S'cool Moves for Learning — Laterality

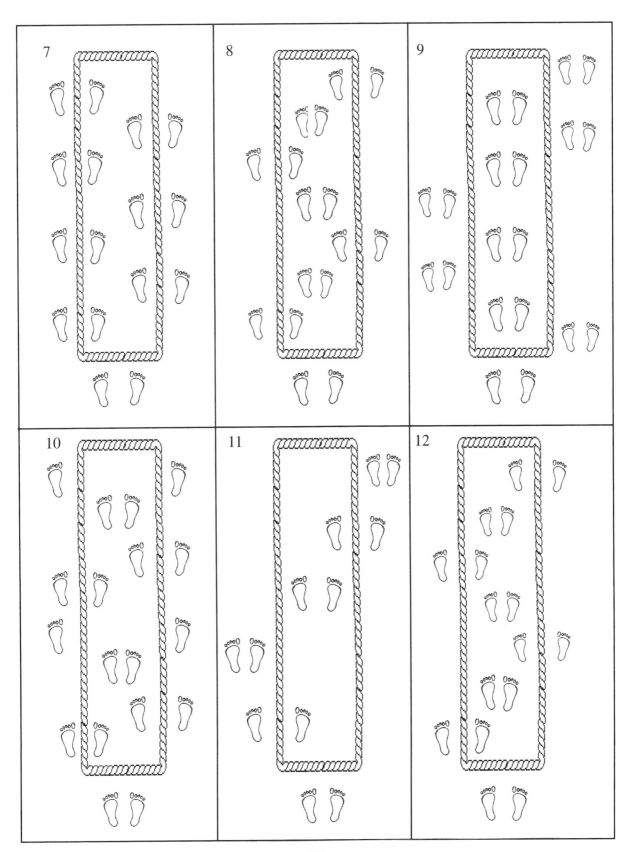

97

Hopping Activities

Activity Description
Hopping activities can be done using the carpet square format, rope activities, or simply hopping in place.

Activity Progression
Begin with the child hopping on one foot while holding a chair for balance. Progress to hopping onto carpet squares and finally working with simple rope patterns. The child should be able to hop in place on either foot many times without losing his balance.

Compensating Behavior
The child may need to wobble to maintain balance, hook one leg around the other leg, or need extra arm and body movement. The child may need to stop frequently to regain balance.

Skipping

Activity Description
The child skips with alternating arms and legs. There should be a nice flow and tempo to the skip.

Activity Progression
Begin with the child hopping in place on each foot. Then ask the child to hop on each foot several times while moving forward. Use verbal commands to help the child switch legs. For instance, the child may hop five times on one leg, and then be instructed to "switch" and hop five times on the other foot. Reduce the number of hops on each foot until the child can hop while alternating each foot. Add opposing arms with the skipping motion.

Compensating Behavior
The child may not use alternating arms and legs, or lack flow and rhythm. The child may use a gallop step instead of a skip. If skipping is difficult, teach each part separately as described, until the child can put it all together. If all lower level movement patterns can be done, skipping should come together easily for the child.

S'cool Moves for Learning

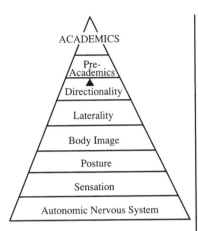

"At about the age of seven, as a result of the further development of the neurons, the social influences of school and increasing pressure to develop verbal thought, many children learn to apply their internal directionality to the outside world... The individual is able to relinquish being the center of the universe and accept an outside center."

Dr. Leela C. Zion
The Physical Side of Learning

Chapter 9

Directionality: Knowing the Left From the Right and Other Directional Terms

- Chart of Behavior Review: Directionality
- Student Profile: Directionality
- Strategies for Success: Directionality
- Integrative Movements and Activities
  Modify Angel Taps, Robo-Pats, and Carpet Squares
  The Clock Game

S'cool Moves for Learning *Directionality*

Chart of Behavior Review: Directionality

❏ does not finish work
❏ difficulty forming letters and numbers
❏ reversal of letters or numbers
❏ stressful reading
❏ writing from bottom-up
❏ writing on one side of paper
❏ writing very small, large, uphill, downhill
❏ writes with no space between words

Others
❏ difficulty with directions of "right" and "left"
❏ difficulty with directional activities when involved in dance, movement, and sports

This page may be reproduced and used to monitor behavior of individual students.

Student Profile: Directionality

Henry is almost eight years old. He stays in from recess often to finish his work because he is slow to complete his assignments. Henry writes his letters from bottom to top and is constantly reversing letters and numbers. Mom works with Henry every night on his printing. He runs his letters together with no space between words. Reading is extremely stressful. Henry reads in a word-by-word fashion and frequently loses his place, even when he uses his finger or bookmark under each line. Music and dance are hard for Henry. He cannot follow directions with rhythm sticks, and always seems to be moving in the opposite direction of everyone else.

Henry would benefit from directionality movement activities that provide opportunities for him to understand positions in space: right, left, above, below, between, next to, in front and behind. Henry may also have laterality problems that need addressing before participating in directionality activities. Many of the movement activities in this chapter build on laterality. To correct directionality problems, Henry must have an internal sense of positions in space while using his body as the reference point. If Henry can complete the laterality movements, then this chapter is the place to begin working with him to improve his academic problems.

Henry's mom or dad could help at home by including in the course of regular conversation words that describe positions in space, emphasizing directionality concepts. They could also play fun games such as back writing to improve directionality. Any family member or friend can play this game with Henry to help him with his reversals. The family member writes a letter or number on Henry's back. Henry writes the letter or number on a large sheet of paper in front of him. This can be done while sitting or standing. Letters and numbers are written one at a time and not mixed; either the child plays with letters at one time or plays with numbers. Some moms and dads remember when they would play back writing with their own parents. Some of the old stuff is still good stuff!

Strategies for Success: Directionality

✓ When giving instruction, use the words "Right," "Left," "Above," "Below," "In front," "Behind," and "Next to." For example. "Place the scissors in the right corner above your name plate."

✓ Letter and number reversals may become a problem for some students. Some reversals are expected for kindergarten and first grade children. The best way to handle reversals is to hold expectations for correct writing of letters and numbers while giving the child strategies to help with reversals. Tape a visual on the desk that looks something like this:

b   butterfly

d   dog

The child is expected to look at the visual when in doubt as to which way the letters or numbers go. Teaching the child the correct way, from the start, eliminates the constant reinforcement of the child writing it wrong, over and over again. Teachers will ask a child, "What's wrong with that d?" when it's facing the wrong way. The child is tipped off that the letter is facing the wrong way, simply erases it and turns it around. No learning has really taken place. Nagging has little effect on correcting reversals. Holding high expectations has a much better outcome. A teacher can say to a child, "I know you are a bit confused on your b's and d's so I've made this helper for you. When in doubt, look here. I'm sure you can write it correctly. From now on, I will expect you to correct this yourself without my assistance."

✓ Some literature suggests that reversals are normal until the end of first grade. This may be true due to confusion rather than any real problem. If midway through the first grade, a child is confused, it would be appropriate to provide the strategies discussed above. The problems will be corrected much faster than allowing the students to write incorrectly throughout their first grade year. Moving into cursive earlier than third grade may help some students with reversal difficulties. During cursive, letters frequently reversed are linked to other letters and more clearly distinguished from one another. Cursive requires different brain processing than printing and is easier for some children.[1]

✓ Tie ribbons or place stickers on the right or left wrists to help children learn their left and right easier. Use a red ribbon or sticker for the right side.

✓ Children may write from the bottom and go up. This habit originates from the desire to start writing closer to the body or needing the line spacing for more accurate perception of where to start and end. The bottom line is an easier starting point than the top line, and less precision in writing is needed when starting at the bottom. This should improve as body image and directionality improve.

✓ Right- and left-handed students should not sit directly next to each other as it crowds both their writing spaces (elbows bumps into each other).

✓ Be careful of desk placement with children experiencing directionality difficulties. If possible, face all children's desk in the same direction so all students have the same perspective of front, back, left, and right.

✓ Get involved in Bal-A-Vis-X, originated by Bill Hubert, a middle school teacher (see reference section). Since S'cool Moves was originally published in 2000, this program has been successfully used with S'cool Moves activities and stations. Children enjoy performing bean bag and ball routines. Children become more motivated and excited about learning while working through the Bal-A-Vis-X Program.

Integrative Movements and Activities

Modify Angel Taps, Robo-Pats, and Carpet Squares

Modify Angel Taps and Robo-Pats with directionality tasks by calling out the names of the limbs to be lifted. Call out, "Right arm," "Left leg," "Right leg," "Left arm." Have the child name the limbs as they are lifted. Number the limbs and call out the numbers, "Lift 1 and 3," "Lift 2 and 4." Give the limbs names of colors, words, or shapes.

Review Carpet Squares and increase directionality skill by calling out the positions in space (right, left, above, below, next to, etc.)

The Clock Game

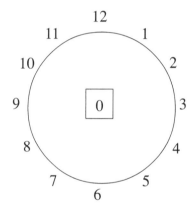

Activity Description
While standing at the board, the child points or draws, from the zero starting point to the numbers on the clock, as the instructor calls out numbers. [2]

Activity Progression
Instruct the child to place the right hand on one of the numbers and the left hand on a second number. Then ask him to move the left hand to a prescribed number and the right hand to another prescribed number that is called out for him. He should move both hands simultaneously, and they should arrive at their respective numbers at the same time. Next, have the child start with each hand on a number on the circle and have him bring both hands to the center at the same time. Reverse the pattern and have the child move his hands from the zero outward to two numbers on the clock. Finally, have the child draw a line from the outer numbers to the center and from the center to the outer numbers. Use numbers directly opposing one another at the beginning and progress to more complex combinations. Use less numbers for younger children.

Compensating Behavior
Both hands should move at the same time and arrive at their destination at the same time. The head should not lean away from the midline of the body. The child may move his body to one side of the clock, avoiding the midline of the body. The face and body may be tense. The child may lean on the board and be unable to keep himself arm's length from the board.

S'cool Moves for Learning

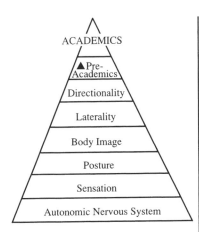

"Of course, we know that our brains are encased in our skulls and are in ceaseless communication with the rest of our bodies. But in practice—when we think about thinking, when we try to encourage it, to mold conditions favorable to learning and creative thought— we tend to regard it as a kind of disembodied process, as if the body's role in that process were to carry the brain from place to place so it can do the important work of thinking."

Dr. Carla Hannaford
Smart Moves

Chapter 10

Pre-Academics: Integrating the Auditory, Visual, and Kinesthetic Systems for Learning

- Chart of Behavior Review: Pre-Academics
- Student Profile: Pre-Academics
- Strategies for Success: Pre-Academics
  Auditory
  Vision
  Eye-Hand Coordination
- Auditory-Visual-Motor Activities
  Listening Ears
  Drum
  Clapping-Tapping Game
- Vision Activities
  Prone Vision Tracking
  Partner Vision 8's
  One Minute Vision Tracking
  Palming
- Eye-Hand Coordination and Visual-Motor Activities
  Squiggles
  Paper Crumpling (PC's)
  Rabbit Ears
  OK's
  Sit and Pats
  Palm Reversals
  Catching and Tossing

Chart of Behavior Review: Pre-Academics

- ❏ awkward pencil grip
- ❏ does not finish work
- ❏ difficulty forming letters and numbers
- ❏ everything is boring
- ❏ off-task
- ❏ reversal of letters or numbers
- ❏ stressful reading
- ❏ writing from bottom-up
- ❏ writing very light or dark
- ❏ writing very small, large, uphill, downhill
- ❏ writes with no space between words

Others
- ❏ difficulty copying from the board
- ❏ writing is physically difficult
- ❏ tires while doing academic tasks
- ❏ easily distracted from academic tasks
- ❏ difficulty doing more than one thing at a time
- ❏ auditory, visual, and kinesthetic skills are not integrated; stressed when processing through all sensory channels

This page may be reproduced and used to monitor behavior of individual students.

Student Profile: Pre-Academics

Timothy is a bright boy who is not able to express his intelligence as easily as other children in the class. The physical act of writing is difficult for him. Tracking from the board to the paper takes him twice as long as the other children in the room. His reading is slow and labored. Timothy maintains a high level of stress as he struggles to keep up with his peers, though cognitive tests show he has the potential to be at the top of his class. He has trouble catching and hitting a ball. He can do one thing at a time well, but becomes bogged down when asked to do more than one thing at a time. Timothy is having a difficult time integrating the visual, auditory, and kinesthetic systems needed for efficient processing in the classroom.

Timothy and all the students we have profiled in previous chapters, should have thorough hearing and vision screenings, including listening therapy assessments and visual processing assessments (see chapter 11 for interviews with specialists in these fields). Timothy would benefit from the movement activities in this chapter. Timothy should be asked to do the movements in the previous chapters to ensure there are no other underlying physical reasons for his difficulties.

The pre-academic level includes auditory-motor and visual-motor activities. "Auditory-motor" combines hearing with movement. "Visual-motor" means to take in information through vision and produce a movement response, such as copying a pattern on paper. "Auditory-visual-motor" refers to using auditory-motor and visual-motor skills together. For instance, repeating a clapping sequence uses vision (seeing the pattern) and audition (hearing the pattern). The auditory- and visual-motor skills are put together with a movement response to complete the pattern. There are many books that cover activities to improve these areas. This chapter includes specific activities to foster improvement in the least amount of time.

Strategies for Success: Pre-Academics

Auditory
✓ Children need to have their hearing checked at birth and routinely once starting school, especially if they have experienced ear infections. Hearing difficulties are often diagnosed once a child is experiencing failure in school. Early detection of hearing difficulties greatly improves a child's chance for success. Many children experiencing difficulty in language arts have had chronic ear infections.

✓ Give instructions before handing out work so that minimal interruptions will be needed once the children start working.

✓ Give instructions one step at a time and ask for verbal repetition of instructions for those students who have auditory sequencing difficulties.

✓ The quieter the teacher talks, the more the children listen. As the teacher's voice becomes louder, so do the children's voices.

✓ Some children do not have the ability to tune out unwanted auditory distractions. The ability to tune in to what is important and tune out unwanted noise is called "auditory figure-ground." For children with auditory figure-ground difficulties, allowing them to listen to calming classical music through headphones while doing seat work helps them focus by providing a consistent calming background.

✓ Have all the students do Listening Ears (covered in this chapter) for better listening skills and attention to verbal directions.

Vision
✓ Much has been written about activities to improve vision. See the reference section under Kaplan, Dennison, and Hannaford for more information.

✓ Keep a close watch for signs of children needing glasses. Be sure to have the nurse screen any child with suspected vision difficulties. Poor vision is one of the most common problems leading to academic difficulties and is often overlooked until the child is in the middle grades.

✓ Remember that the younger the reader, the larger the print should be. This is especially true for children who have difficulty tracking.

✓ Printing reading passages on colored or distracting backgrounds makes it difficult for children to pick out the letters from the background. White paper with black letters is the easiest for children to read.

✓ Remind children to sit straight in their chairs and keep their head in line with their shoulders while reading and writing.

✓ Warm-up the children for reading by doing simple tracking activities or Figure 8's. Do Rhythmic Tapping including tapping around the eye area. Take vision breaks and have children blink, look at their noses, move their eyes in all directions, breathe deeply, and do some palming.

✓ A child's vision may play a factor in the ability to write well. If writing improves by placing the paper closer or farther away, suspect focus problems. Check to see if writing improves when standing or when the child is writing at arm's length. If it does, allow the child to write in that manner, when appropriate, until the vision concerns are remedied.

✓ Make yawning good manners! Yawning relaxes tension in the jaw and facial area while waking up nerves to the brain that help with vision. When children begin to get tired or bored, have them pretend to be loud animals in the zoo and make animal sounds while yawning big. Massage the joint that moves while opening and closing the mouth (right by the ear, referred to as the temporal-mandibular joint, TMJ). Have children make long drawn-out vowel sounds while yawning. For fun, have children choose the vowel they want to use. This makes for interesting sounds and harmonizing.

✓ Have the children do neck rolls to relieve tension in the neck. The children touch their chin to their chest and then gently roll to one side and the other. Roll the neck side to the side and not to the back (too much stress).

Eye-Hand Coordination

✓ Don't underestimate the power of a correct pencil grip to improve writing performance. Here's a way to teach the correct pencil grip: have the child hold his pencil with the nondominant hand, the eraser pointing toward the ceiling. The writing hand pinches or hugs the pencil using the index finger and thumb. Tell the child to put the pencil to sleep (lay it in the nook or webbing between the index finger and thumb) and put a pillow under its head (with the middle finger). Reinforce proper grip and make a big deal out of using a good grip. Take surprise photos and put children in the pencil grip hall of fame. Purchased pencil grips can be used to guide children in proper finger placement. The grips are made from rubber or soft spongy material and come in different shapes. Let the child decide which type is most comfortable.

✓ Tactile awareness activities to improve writing include manipulating different textures, massaging the fingers and wrists, and shaking out the wrists. Allow the child to stop writing periodically to relax the fingers and wrists.

✓ Limit copying from the board or copying words that are posted on a bulletin board (word walls). Make word lists available at the child's desk.

✓ Allow children experiencing writing difficulties to sit on the floor and write on a firm surface such as a clipboard. This helps the child compensate for balance, kinesthetic, and postural difficulties.

✓ When teaching letter formation, first teach it with gross motor activities (tracing in air, making the letters with the body, etc.). After letters are formed easily, work with forming letters with large utensils such as paintbrushes, large chalk, large markers, or large crayons. When making the transition to paper, be sure the paper has large lines, initially. Spacing may be taught by having children hold their space with their pinkies between words. Gradually reduce the line spacing as children are able to write easily within bigger lines.

Auditory-Visual-Motor Activities

Most primary teachers understand the importance of strengthening the auditory-visual-motor system. Their students actively participate in rhythm and sequencing activities using instruments, sounds, marching, Simon Says, word plays, and songs. These are great to do along with the movement activities in this chapter.

Listening Ears

Movement Description
With the thumb and index fingers, have the child pull the ears gently back and uncurl the ear lobes using a massaging action. Begin at the top of the ear lobe and massage to the bottom lobe. This activity helps focus attention on hearing and relaxes tension in the cranial bones. The child's ability to tune-in to relevant information improves. Do Listening Ears before playing auditory-visual-motor games and activities or when better listening is needed.

Movement Progression
Have the child turn the head from side to side while doing Listening Ears to release any neck tension that can affect hearing. Before doing the activity, notice which side is hearing more sound. Notice again after the activity. Is the hearing more balanced? Are sounds more clear?

Compensating Behavior
Children with hearing difficulties may read lips without realizing they are doing so. To check this out, the teacher may gradually hold a piece of paper over his mouth while talking with the child. Watch for changes in understanding or signs of stress. The child may watch other children before responding to instructions, or there may be a delay in responding to auditory input.

Drum
Activity Description
The drum activity develops the auditory-motor system only. The vision is not added to this activity. The assistant stands behind the seated child so that she cannot watch the pattern being tapped. With a small drum, tap out simple patterns. Hand the drum to the child and ask for a repeat of the pattern. If a drum is not available, the patterns may be clapped out.

Activity Progression
Progress to more involved patterns. Add background noise or music to improve auditory figure-ground.

Compensating Behavior
Notice head turning to one side when listening to others and also note which ear seems to be preferred for listening.

Clapping-Tapping Game

Activity Description
Demonstrate several taps (T) by tapping the table top with both hands. Label the action as "Tapping" (T). Demonstrate several claps (C). Label the action as "Clapping." Say, "We are going to play a clapping-tapping game. I will do it first. Then I want you to do it. Watch carefully so I don't trick you." Use the following patterns to integrate the auditory-visual-motor systems. Hyphens (-) indicate a two-second pause. TC, TCT, CCTC, TT-C, C-CC, CTCCT, TC-CT, C-TCT, TTC-C, C-T-TC. Follow these patterns or make up patterns as you go. Give the child several opportunities to repeat the patterns correctly.

Activity Progression
Begin with the simple patterns and progress to the more difficult patterns as success is observed. Have the child make up patterns.

Activity Compensation
The child may be slow to respond or doesn't wait to hear the pattern. The taps and claps may be very loud for more kinesthetic feedback.

Vision Activities

Prone Vision Tracking
Activity Description
Have the child lie on his back so the trunk and neck do not have to work against the force of gravity. The child will track objects while in this position. Vision activities should not be more than a few minutes in length. The eyes tire easily. More is not better in this case.

Activity Progression
While lying on the floor, have the child follow a large object (his

hand works best initially, then a ball or toy) with his eyes. Once this can be done easily, have the child track small objects, such as a pencil eraser. Using the eyes and hands together can assist tracking. Grasp two hands together with index fingers touching. Follow the object by touching the fingers to the object as it is moving. Next, have the child focus on objects in different positions above and below the midline in the vertical plane, as well as on the sides of the body in the horizontal plane. Finally, hold a small tube or cup in different positions and ask the child to place the index fingers inside the tube or cup as it moves through different planes. Be sure to have the child move the arms back to midline after tracking each time. After these activities can be done in a lying position, progress to doing them in a sitting position.

Compensating Behavior
The child may avoid the midline by leaning the head to one side of the body. One eye may close to avoid tracking with both eyes. The child may keep her hands close to the object that she is focusing on to keep from having to refocus her eyes. The child may maintain stress through tense body muscles or grasping the chair with the hands. The child may want to lean the head back as the target is moved closer to the eyes. The tongue may follow the eyes. This can be felt by putting a hand under the chin.

Partner Vision 8's

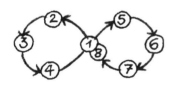

Activity Description
If children are older than 9, partner them with a tracking buddy. They face one another and act as if they are going to shake hands. Once the hands are together, they pull back just a bit so the fingers are grasping, rather than the palms. The thumbs are in the "thumb wrestling" position, with the partner's thumbs touching each others. The partners move their hands together in a Figure 8 pattern. One person tracks the 8 while the other person observes. When the child loses focus, the partner taps on the thumb to bring the child's focus back to the thumb. Remember to add stickers to the thumb to help with tracking. Track using right, then left hands. A minute or two for each partner is plenty of time for this activity.

> *"Vision is a lifetime supply of fun."*
> *"My eyes swim like dolphins through the waters of books."*
>
> from fourth grade students whose goals were to improve their vision for better reading ability

Minute Moves!

One-Minute Vision Tracking

Activity Description

Put the basic elements of vision tracking into one simple procedure with the following exercises. Use a small ball the size of a racquetball. This is by no means a replacement for vision therapy, but it does help those children needing a vision tracking tune-up.

Convergence: Move the ball straight toward the child's nose to a comfortable point; not too close. The child should not see double. Move the ball away from the nose. Repeat three times.

Near to Far and Far to Near Focus: Move the ball in a straight line toward the child's nose then move it in a downward arc away from the nose, at arm's length away. Repeat three times. Reverse the movement and take the ball away from the nose in a straight line and then bring it in a downward arc toward the nose. Repeat three times.

Side to Side and Up and Down Tracking: Have the child watch the ball as it moves at eye level from the left side to the right side, and from the right side to the left side, checking for comfortable midline crossing (the point where the eyes meet in the center above the nose). Repeat three times. Move the ball up and down at the midline. Repeat three times.

Circular Tracking: Have the child watch the ball while it is moved clockwise in a circle, and then counterclockwise once, keeping it within a comfortable field of vision—arm's length.

Figure 8's: Have the child watch the ball while it is moved in the Figure 8 pattern.

Palming

Activity Description

Have the child rub the hands together until the palms are warm, then gently cover his closed eyes with the palms of the hands. Overlap the fingers above the bridge of the nose to create as much darkness as possible. Keep the eyes covered for a minute or two, counting between twenty and fifty breaths. Ask the child if he sees any colors as he looks into the darkness of his hands. The palming action is triple-duty in that it revives the eyes, increases blood flow to the hands for writing, and provides quiet time for the mind.

Eye-Hand Coordination and Visual-Motor Activities

Squiggles

Activity Description
If a child has balance difficulties, squiggles may be done at an easel or on the board at arm's length, before progressing to doing them seated at a desk. If the child prefers, squiggles may be done while sitting on the floor. For floor and desk work, provide the child with a large half sheet piece of newspaper or large paper with a colored squiggle on it, taped to the desk, or held by the child's knee if on the floor.

For young children, place a star at the left side of the squiggle where the child should begin. With a marker that is a different color than the pattern drawn, the child draws over the squiggle, from left to right, as quickly as possible. The child should not trace slowly. The first few attempts may be inaccurate. Encourage the child to try again until she gets the pattern correct. Repeat ten times. Have the child copy the squiggle on her own to develop visual memory. Always encourage correct pencil grip, good posture, and maintaining the paper at the visual field midline. The eyes should watch the hands to improve eye-hand coordination. Begin squiggles standing at arm's length from the paper or board and then progress to sitting at a desk.[1]

Activity Progression
Initially, the child may need to trace the squiggles with her dominant hand to get kinesthetic information. After this is done easily, do the patterns as described above. Progress from the simple to the more complex squiggles. For added fun, have the child do squiggles with markers in both hands. The hands mirror one another and move in a continuous flow making loops that are drawn while moving the hands in and out from the midline of the body. This is free form and no pattern is needed. The child can squiggle moving vertically down the length of the paper.

Beginning Squiggles   Challenging Squiggles

Compensating Behavior
Midline avoidance is observed when the head or body leans away from the midline. The paper may gradually move away from the midline of the body, and the body may lean away from the writing area. When eyes close or look away while drawing the pattern, there may be eye-hand coordination difficulties.

Paper Crumpling (PC's)

Activity Description
After completing squiggles, have the child stand with her dominant hand down at one side and hold the paper by the corner in the dominant hand. The child crumples the paper quickly, keeping her arm straight at her side and using only her fingers to crumple the paper.

Activity Progression
For added challenge, crumple paper with the nondominant hand but only after the dominant hand is adept and the fine motor skills needed for writing are in place.

Compensating Behavior
The arm will want to be raised, calling in muscles of the forearm and shoulders, or even the whole body. The other hand may attempt to help out. The opposite side of the body may be tense. The tongue may stick out of the mouth and the face display tension while the paper is crumpled. As proficiency develops, overflow tension should decrease. The body, face, and opposing arm should remain relaxed while the dominant side crumples the paper.

Rabbit Ears

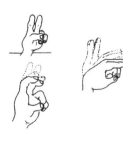

Activity Description
The child places the elbow of her dominant hand on the table while making the letter "V" with the first and second fingers. The ring and pinky fingers are bent and covered by the thumb. The "V" fingers bend several times at the knuckles. Next, the assistant bends his hand up and down at the wrist several times saying, "Bend your wrist like this to make your rabbit say hello." The child repeats the activity several times.

Compensating Behavior
The child may not be able to move the wrist in isolation and hold the thumb and fingers in position while moving the wrist. This may

indicate a difficulty with timing and sequencing. The child may show muscle fatigue in the wrist by not being able to repeat the movement several times. The child may have to place the fingers in the correct position and think about how to do the position.

OK's

Activity Description
Have the child begin with her thumb and index finger touching one another. The child touches each finger to her thumb, ending with the pinky and thumb touching one another. Make sure that the thumb touches the tips of the fingers when making the circle with the thumb and finger. The child repeats the activity, touching all fingers to the thumb for several sequences without stopping. Repeat this movement with each hand separately. Do this movement with eyes open and then with eyes closed.

Activity Progression
After the child masters this activity with one hand and with eyes open and closed, progress to doing the activity with both hands at the same time. Once this is done with eyes open, repeat the activity with eyes closed.

Compensating Behavior
The child may slouch over, supporting the body with the free hand. There may be overflow to the other hand when working just one hand. The child may be unable to touch each finger to the thumb. The body and face may be tense. The child may have to look at the hand to accomplish the task. The circle that is made with the finger and the thumb may be flat.

Sit and Pats

Activity Description
Sitting in a chair with hands on his lap, the child copies the patterns patted by the assistant.

Activity Progression
Increase the level of difficulty by changing the rhythm. Start with a basic pattern of two pats on each thigh. Proceed to a pattern of two pats on one thigh and one pat on the other thigh. Add listening and talking to the pattern before moving on to a more difficult pattern. Sing while spelling out words. Use the melody of favorite, known songs and replace the words with spelling words. For example,

spell and sing "because" to the alphabet song tune. Singing is a wonderful integrating activity for the brain and helps children remember much easier than just saying the words. Sit and Pats can be done any time during the day to add rhythm practice to daily activities. For an added challenge, have the children repeat the following pattern: pat once on their thighs then cross their arms over and pat once opposite hands to opposite thighs, uncross the arms and pat once and end with a clap (pat, cross over, pat, clap). Repeat the sequence in a rhythmic fashion. This is fun to do to songs with a good beat.

Compensating Behavior
The child may be able to keep the pattern going only when tension is built up in the body. The elbows should remain bent and the hands held above the lap by a few inches. When adding listening and talking, the child may lose the pattern.

Palm Reversals
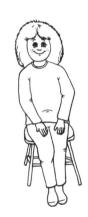
Activity Description
The assistant is seated in a chair with palms facing down on the lap. The child is in the same position. She follows the assistant as the palms are flipped up and down, alternating hands and sometimes flipping both hands at the same time.

Activity Progression
Make the patterns more difficult and allow the child to lead the activity.

Compensating Behavior
The body and face may tense while attempting the movement. The child may need to look intensely at the palm to accomplish the task, or be unable to keep the palms on his lap, and compensate by holding the palms out alongside the body.

Catching and Tossing

Activity Description
Have the child perform simple catching and tossing activities. If the child has a protective reaction to catching, start with a scarf, balloon, or large soft rubber ball until the reaction is gone. Proceed from larger to smaller items to throw and catch. Start at a close distance to the target and gradually move further away.

118

S'cool Moves for Learning

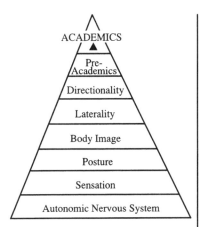

"All the best educational programs around the world combine elements that stimulate both a child's physical and mental development–for in truth there is no split between the two."

Gordon Dryden and Dr. Jeannette Vos
The Learning Revolution

Chapter 11

Academics: Putting All the Pieces Together

- Student Profile: Academics
- Strategies for Success: Academics
- Integrating Academics into S'cool Moves for Learning: A Matter of Creativity
- Tying up Loose Ends—Talking with Specialists
  What do I do if a child does not have a dominant hand?
  Why is writing a difficult task for some children?
  How is listening important to academic success?
  Does visual processing play an important role in academic success?
  Why do some children have a difficult time staying focused and motivated?

Student Profile: Academics

Melody was assessed by the school psychologist and scored in the above-average range in intelligence. Her teachers say that she is very bright, but that something is holding her back from putting all the pieces of the learning puzzle together. Melody's processing is slow. To compound her difficulties, she is a perfectionist and will not turn in assignments until they are done neatly and without error. Melody's reading teacher suspected that she was experiencing visual processing difficulties causing her reading and writing to be slow. An assessment by an optometrist specializing in vision therapy confirmed her teacher's suspicions. Melody joined a small group of classmates who were participating in S'cool Moves for Learning and developed her visual processing skills, improving her performance in all areas of the Learning Pyramid. Within two months, her reading fluency speed doubled, and she was completing her work faster. Her grades at the first reporting period were A's and B's. The parents were encouraged to have Melody re-examined by the optometrist to be sure the processing difficulties were improving. Melody might benefit from completing a vision therapy program in the summer if she still has difficulties.

This chapter helps children who lack organization at the academic level. Children are required to do many things simultaneously in the course of the regular school day. For example, they must listen to the teacher, write on command, respond to questions, and process information through the visual, auditory, and kinesthetic systems. Ideally, students will reach a point where they can process information through all sensory channels easily, with energy left for higher level thinking.

Toward the end of the chapter, we interview specialists who share their perspectives and expertise in the areas of writing, listening, vision, and behavior.

Strategies for Success: Academics

✓ The book, *The Learning Revolution* by Gordon Dryden and Jeannette Vos (1999) is a compilation of innovative programs to help children who are behind, academically. Specialized kinesiology, the field that utilizes movement to improve learning, was listed in the top ten best "catch-up" programs.

✓ Keep up on the hottest areas in science today, the neurosciences, and apply the latest research to the classroom.

✓ Read *The Out-of-Sync Child* by Carol Stock Kranowitz (1998) for a full discussion of Sensory Integration (SI) Dysfunction. The book offers comprehensive information on recognizing the signs of SI difficulties and strategies to help children be successful in the school setting.

✓ Be aware at any one grade level there may be a three year difference in normal developmental patterns between the faster and the slower developing child.

✓ Help children organize themselves by providing a ziplock plastic bag containing everything they need on a daily basis: pencil (regular or fat), crayons (regular or fat), markers, highlighters, erasers, and rulers. Inventory the bag at the end of the day and provide time to sharpen pencils and restock any items that need replacing or are missing. Daily, provide time for students to organize the items in their desks. Missing homework and late papers are usually found in the black hole of students' desks.

✓ Children need the movement break recess provides. Limit keeping children in at recess to complete assignments. Some schools have after-school homework programs that require children who do not get their homework done to attend the program.

✓ For a thorough understanding of the movement-learning connection, read *Smart Moves* by Carla Hannaford (1995). Her book discusses the physiological basis of learning, and builds solid theory supporting body-mind integration.

Integrating Academics into S'cool Moves for Learning: A Matter of Creativity

Students in kindergarten through second grade are usually challenged enough by the movement activities that they do not need the added stress of integrating academics. However, there are times when adding academic elements can be fun for primary students. Below are a few ways this can be done in the primary grades.

- During movement activities, have children recite the alphabet, count aloud, or sing their favorite songs.

- If children are just learning the alphabet, hold up large, colorful flash cards of alphabet letters with pictures to match. Have students read the flash cards while doing appropriate activities or movements.

- During carpet squares activities, place alphabet letters, numbers, or sight words in the corner of each square, and have children jump into the square as the letter, number, or word is called. For sequencing, give more than one instruction at a time. Have children hold in their mind two, three, and four commands at a time such as, "Jump into the square that has the alphabet letter a, then c, then f."

Integrate academics after children have accomplished movements without compensating behavior. The most effective way to add academics is to have the children learn their spelling words, new vocabulary, phonics lessons, or math facts during movement activities.

The following activities for older students require a word wall, a rubber ball large enough to bounce easily, a balance board, and a Marsden Ball (explained on page 123).

<u>Sit and Pats with a Word Wall</u>
Be sure the child can do Sit and Pats well, before adding academics. Place the child in a chair in front of a word wall (a bulletin board with words stapled to it). As the child does Sit and Pats, he reads or spells the words on the wall while maintaining the rhythm of two pats per side.

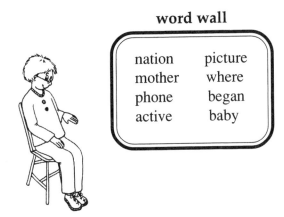

word wall

nation	picture
mother	where
phone	began
active	baby

Marsden Ball Activities
A Marsden Ball can be purchased through a vision therapy supplier (see references). The Marsden Ball is a small ball with letters printed on it that hangs on a string from the ceiling or on a hook suspended from the wall. The child hits the ball in a rhythmic and controlled manner, while visually tracking the ball. Vision therapy books have many activities that can be done with the Marsden Ball. The child may hit the ball with his hand or use a specially designed bat for the activities. For the classroom, the Marsden Ball activities are done in a standing position. To add academics, the assistant holds flash cards up in front of the child and asks him to track back and forth from the flash cards to the Marsden Ball while saying the words, or reciting the math facts on the flash cards. Children enjoy Marsden Ball activities and forget they are doing academics. In their minds, they are playing! Perfect!

For an added challenge, a balance board may be used while hitting the Marsden Ball. Purchase balance boards through vision therapy and physical therapy suppliers. Children enjoy the challenge of using a balance board and usually do quite well with it, if they do not have balance difficulties. It is important to keep the Marsden Ball activities controlled and rhythmic. There is a tendency for this activity to get sloppy, reducing its effectiveness.

Rubber Ball with Academics
Be sure the child can bounce a ball easily and rhythmically before adding academics. With a large, rubber ball, have the child bounce the ball with the dominant hand while reading, spelling, or reciting math facts from the word wall. Progress to using the nondominant hand, alternating between hands, and bouncing the ball in a circle.

One note of caution: bouncing the ball can become loud and distracting to other children.

Two programs integrate nicely with the academic portion of S'cool Moves for Learning. Read Kwik:Learn Quick (see references) is a program for decoding words quickly using common chunks, prefixes, and suffixes. The skills transfer to spelling quite nicely. Words from the program can be used for the word wall, though any words will work. The program includes visual tracking worksheets to help students track left to right and recognize the word chunks quickly.

Five Minutes to Better Reading Skills (see references) trains visual processing through the use of timed phonics drills. Children scan the phonetic words from left to right as quickly as they can, while being timed for one minute. The children graph their results for each lesson and move on to the next drill once they have accomplished a word-per-minute fluency based on their age, with less than five errors. There are forty-two lessons in the program. In five minutes a day, this program trains visual processing and automatic word recognition extremely well.

Integrate Bal-A-Vis-X (see reference section) into academic and physical education programs. As discussed in the directionality chapter, this program is a highly effective way to motivate struggling students and yields impressive gains in academics.

For more information on how S'cool Moves has been adapted throughout the years, read our newest spiral book titled *Minute Moves for the Classroom.* Teachers have contributed to this book, and explain how they have made S'cool Moves part of their day.

A S'cool Moves music and movement book and video is currently in production and should be released in 2003.

There are many powerful programs that help children experiencing difficulties in the academic areas. Blend the movement activities in this program with your current academic curricula. There are no right or wrong answers. Experiment! Play! Enjoy!

Tying Up Loose Ends—Talking With Specialists

The remainder of this chapter is dedicated to answering questions that teachers commonly ask during inservices. We will discuss dominance, writing, listening, vision, and behavior as they relate to children in the classroom. To fully answer these questions, we asked specialists in various fields to share their perspectives and expertise. We begin this section with hand dominance and a commonly asked question.

What do I do if a child does not have a dominant hand?

Hand dominance develops after laterality has been established. When a child is having difficulty determining a preferred hand, laterality has not been established. Hand dominance begins appearing around the age of two.[1] Prior to this time, the child uses his hands alternately, and appears to have no consistent choice. Determining a child's dominant hand can be tricky. No one wants to be responsible for pushing a child into using one hand or the other. Through observation, assessment, and dominance activities, children may be guided to discover their dominant hand for themselves.

Elizabeth Davies was a specialist in perceptual-motor training and discussed her perspective on hand dominance during week-long training sessions. The information on dominance in this chapter is from Mrs. Davies' workshops.

When a child has difficultly determining a dominant hand, assess which hand tends to be preferred with the following activities:

- Ask her which way she brushes her teeth, up, down, or side to side (it's a silly question to see what hand they use).
- At the board, ask her to make circles while holding markers in each hand. The circle that looks more round and controlled was made with the dominant hand.
- Walk a bean bag up her back and ask her to grab it quickly with one hand when it gets to her neck.
- Have her throw at a target as hard as she can. Do this with each hand. Observe which hand is more accurate.
- Toss the bean bag on the ground, a few yards in front of her while tossing to alternate sides of the body. Say, "Quickly run

and get the bean bag and bring it back to me using only one hand." Observe which hand is used. When the bean bag is thrown to her left, does she use her left hand? If the bean bag is thrown to her right, does she use her right hand? If so, midline difficulties may be suspected.
- Observe her making Figure 8 patterns with the right hand and the left hand. Usually a dominant side will be evident.
- Observe her throughout the day. Which hand is used more often?

Once you have determined which hand appears to be stronger and more agile, encourage the child to use that hand for cutting, writing, drawing, coloring, etc. Place tools consistently to the side that seems preferred.

If a preferred hand can not be determined, complete laterality activities, Squiggles, and Figure 8's. Encourage activities that do not require writing, such as legos, and allow more time for dominance to be revealed or determined.

Rarely is it thought that the arrangement of students' desks can interfere with developing a preferred hand, but it definitely can. When children's desks are facing one another, they often mirror the person across from them, causing handedness confusion. Sometimes the confusion is brief, but for youngsters already struggling with laterality, this compounds the problem. If at all possible, face all children's desk in the same direction so they have the same perspective of front, back, left, and right. Young children like having their own space and enjoy not being positioned next to another child all the time. One first grade teacher said that facing all the desks forward made a dramatic difference in reversals, hand confusion, and the students' ability to understand directional concepts.

Dominance should be determined by the time a child enters kindergarten. If dominance is not determined by kindergarten, there may be laterality problems. Children who lack dominance by kindergarten should participate in a S'cool Moves for Learning program. Add movement activities from this book to the kindergarten physical education program. So many children would benefit, and the movements are fun for the entire class, including the teacher!

Why is writing a difficult task for some children?

There is a tendency to assume that all students are ready to write regardless of their physiological development. Writing is generally thought of as a fine motor skill requiring only adequate finger and wrist movement Below are the additional physical components needed for writing.[2]

> **S**table postural muscles. The muscles in front must be as strong as the back muscles. They must both work with equal strength to maintain the trunk and allow the child to write erect and defy gravity. This anchors shoulder and arm movement. Stable shoulder muscles allow the hand to grasp from a stable base.
>
> **A**dequate trunk balance allows a child to move the hands without upsetting sitting balance.
>
> **T**he muscles all along the spine must be well developed to allow for arm movement across the midline of the body without leaning in the direction of the arm movement.
>
> **E**ase of arm rotation is essential to allow correct positioning and shifting of the wrist for writing. The wrist must be free to move to maintain optimal positions for writing.
>
> **T**he trunk, shoulder, forearm, and wrist must move as a coordinated whole. Stability of hand muscles supports well-coordinated finger movements.
>
> **S**ubtle feedback from muscles and the movement system is required to monitor and adjust movement as well as remember past movement experiences so that the child doesn't have to relearn to write each time.
>
> **P**recise timing in muscles work in an opposing manner. As one group relaxes the other must contract.
>
> **G**ood tactile discrimination is needed so the child doesn't have to rely on visual feedback.

Writing is a two-dimensional task combining touch and movement with vision and language.[3] This requires a high degree of integration of the auditory, visual, and kinesthetic systems. A child experiencing difficulties with the integration of any of these systems may encounter writing challenges.

How is listening important to academic success?
Teachers often want children to listen to them and are concerned about childrens' inability to listen. Hearing and listening are two very different processes. Dr. Judith Belk, a speech and language therapist shared her perspective on the importance of listening.

Dr. Belk: The ability to listen, to tune in to what's important and to tune out distractions, is critical to academics and has parallels in vision. This includes screening foreground/background, being selective rather than inundated with incoming data, and being able to regulate effects of stimuli. It is exhausting to have to be so vigilant all the time to protect oneself from the onslaught of what may be perceived as obnoxious or confusing information. One can shut their eyes and not have to see what is around them, but we can not close our ears entirely. They are always "on call." However, you can hear imprecisely, without the precision which comes from purposely tuning in.

Margot: *Is there a connection between reading and listening?*
Dr. Belk: The connection between reading and listening is extremely strong, with increasing numbers of researchers addressing the auditory component of dyslexia, as well as other auditory processing/language problems.

Margot: *How is the physical act of writing related to the auditory system?*
Dr. Belk: The physical act of writing is highly associated with the visual, auditory, and vestibular triad. I find that as clients make gains in their facility to express ideas, their ability to translate a flow of ideas into written form comes more easily. The vestibular system gives feedback about the body's writing posture including the position of fingers, writing implements, and paper, whereas the auditory and visual systems give feedback about order and sequencing of ideas. This triad works together to produce legible writing with coherent, organized ideas.

Margot: *How can schools implement a listening program?*
Dr. Belk: The listening program I would recommend is called SAMONAS, an acronym for "Spectral Activated Music of Optimal Natural Structure." This therapy method has been practiced for many years. The therapy affects the brain and nervous system directly through the sense of hearing. The SAMONAS

method is specially filtered classical music designed to retrain listening skills. Implementing the SAMONAS listening method is relatively easy. One needs a few portable CD players, a number of specifically designed earphones, and the therapeutic CD's. All of this is reusable for a long time, if cared for. Taking 15–20 minutes daily out of instructional time is well worth it for many children. This worked well at a high school last year where children did their program during access period, before school, or during communication skills class. It's pretty easy to find a way to make it work.

Margot: *What kinds of children seem to benefit the most from a listening program?*
Dr. Belk: I suggest you consider students who have the most trouble with attention, focus, information processing, and/or motor coordination. There are some interesting combinations of problems which lend themselves to the use of sensory-based listening programs.

Margot: *Should schools contact an audiologist such as yourself, trained in listening methods, to serve as a consultant to schools wanting to implement a listening program?*
Dr. Belk: Yes, it's helpful to have pre- and post-screening instruments. I would include the IMAS as one of the screening tools.

Results reported by individuals who complete a listening therapy program include:
- decreased sound sensitivity
- increased receptive and expressive language
- improved articulation/speech intelligibility; decreased stuttering
- increased concentration
- decreased hyperactivity
- improved auditory processing
- improved reading and digit span sequential processing
- improved coordination and balance
- increased enjoyment of classical music.

For more information, Dr. Belk recommends *When Listening Comes Alive* (1994), written by Paul Madaule, a man who had extreme learning difficulties in school. Through listening therapy, he overcame his difficulties, opened his own listening center, and wrote this inspiring book.

Does visual processing play an important role in academic success?

We interviewed Dr. Steven Goedert, an optometrist and vision therapist in Redding, California. We asked him some important questions about vision and its role in the classroom.

Debi: *When people refer to vision, they usually refer to the ability to see near and far. What is your definition of vision?*
Dr. Goedert: What you just described is eyesight. Eyesight is the ability to see images clearly at far and near distance. I will quote from Bruce Wolff's work titled *From Sight to Vision*, "Vision is an emergent from eyesight, experience, learning, doing, sequencing, analoging, and visualizing...a holographic paradigm...these ingredients become synonymous with sight, hindsight, foresight, and insight. Vision is past, present, and future. It supersedes time and space. It is a total processing system."

Debi: *Schools rarely take a look at visual processing as it relates to children with learning difficulties. Why is this?*
Dr. Goedert: The conventional concept of vision doesn't take into consideration binocularity, eye teaming, tracking, and how visual information is taken into the brain and processed. This thinking does not acknowledge the dominance of vision in sensory input. Eighty percent of the anatomical afferent neural pathways to the brain are visual.

Debi: *How do vision difficulties affect children's progress in reading, writing, and learning in general?*
Dr. Goedert: Compared to another child with the same academic ability, the child with a visual processing problem has to work a lot harder. Problems with eye focusing and teaming can put higher level visual processes at risk. This would include, but not be limited to, visual memory, visualization, eye-hand coordination, logic, attention, and reversal frequency. One, or a combination of the aforementioned, if not working at expected levels, can adversely reduce classroom performance.

Debi: *Why do you think that vision therapy still remains controversial after years of substantial research validating vision training?*
Dr. Goedert: Understanding vision training as a treatment option requires a cognitive shift to the holistic approach to learn-

ing. Philosophies and beliefs establish how we look upon, interpret, and understand different techniques. Some philosophies are hard to change no matter how much empirical data might be presented to support the efficacy of vision training.

Debi: *What kind of changes do you see in children who go through your vision therapy program?*
Dr. Goedert: I see increased self esteem and confidence in children's abilities to process new and challenging information.

Debi: *What can schools do to provide vision support for children who do not have the resources to pay for vision therapy?*
Dr. Goedert: There are many simple exercises that can be easily taught to educators and can be used to identify and to improve simple visual processing deficits. Whenever possible, I offer these to interested educators.

Debi: *Is it appropriate for school personnel to do some basic vision training with students?*
Dr. Goedert: Yes. Most of these tests and exercises are non-invasive, enjoyable, and easily understood by both teacher and student.

Debi: *Is there anything else you would like people to know about your field?*
Dr. Goedert: Often, simply identifying a visual processing problem can help a child to understand that they can be intelligent and still struggle in school. Identifying a visual problem can also help the teacher and parent understand why this child is not responding to traditional teaching and tutoring techniques. If a child is seeing double every time he reads, and the words run off the page, this is not an intellectual difficulty, but a visual problem. This can be efficiently remedied by vision training, thereby removing a major stumbling block for the child.

Debi: *How important is lighting to how a child functions in school?*
Dr. Goedert: There are many studies that have been done on proper lighting in the classroom. Many people are very sensitive to the restrictive visual light spectrum of fluorescent light. In some individuals, the brain waves are disrupted by fluorescent lights, causing a variety of symptoms ranging from fatigue to nausea.

There are "full- spectrum" fluorescent light bulbs available that give more of the visual spectrum therefore reducing some of the problems with brain wave interference. Natural light is still the best. A good compromise is the "mix" of fluorescent lights with incandescence which provide a broader light spectrum.

Debi: *How can parents and teachers get more information about vision and its effect on learning?*
Dr. Goedert: There is a group, Parents Active for Vision Education (P.A.V.E.) that support parents through education about visual processing difficulties as they relate to learning. They are an active group and recently were instrumental in bringing about the resolution by the National PTA stating that there needs to be earlier detection in public schools for children with visual processing difficulties.

Debi: *What are the indications that a child is developmentally ready to read?*
Dr. Goedert: A child is developmentally ready to read when the eyes can work together locating and tracking near objects without the neck moving or body involvement. This usually takes place around 4 1/2 to 5 1/2 years old. The eyes should be leading the body, not the body leading the eyes. The visual system is part of the whole body. Children that have developed physically, as well as mentally, and are up to developmental norms, usually have few visual processing problems. The visual system is designed to grow and develop with the rest of the body systems. A behavioral eye exam should be done before a child starts reading. Some general areas that are evaluated are oculomotor skills such as eye tracking, teaming, and fusion ability.

Debi: *What may be the result of children who are pushed too early to read?*
Dr. Goedert: Problems can range from double vision (words running off the page or using a finger to keep their place), headaches, drowsiness in class, rubbing the eyes, poor comprehension, omitting or substituting small words, and/or failing to complete work on time. Avoidance behaviors may emerge, such as apparent laziness, resistance to school work, or the onset of hyperactivity. While struggling to overcome these problems, children avoid bothersome tasks or make adaptations in an attempt to reduce the difficulties and discomfort they experience. Many of these chil-

dren function at grade level until the third or fourth grade. At this point, print gets smaller and the demand for reading increases. Poor visual skills are developed by these children in their primary grades, compromising performance as demands increase. A child who might have been a good achiever, now has decreased comprehension and has to really work hard to stay at previous performance levels.

Debi: *What can parents and teachers do to help children become ready to read? Do eye exercises help children develop the eye muscles for reading, even if they are too young to start reading?*
Dr. Goedert: The primary experience a child needs to develop the visual system is direct contact with the physical environment. Incorporate the visual system into everyday activities. Reaching, grasping, jumping, balance, judging distance, and estimating size of objects all help to integrate a child's visual system with the rest of the body. Secondary experiences, such as computers and television, isolate the visual system and are not helpful in creating healthy sensory integration. Real life experiences train the visual system more effectively than isolated eye exercises.

Debi: *If a child isn't ready, yet the school system expects them to be reading by a certain age, what can the teacher do to relieve the stress the child may experience?*
Dr. Goedert: If the teacher recognizes that a child is struggling with visual demands, there are several things that can be done to relieve stress for the child. The teacher should encourage the child to take frequent breaks, do activities involving large muscle groups, create games that involve locating distant targets, train eye movement that facilitate near work (vision tracking exercises), and refer parents to a Behavioral Optometrist before avoidance patterns develop.

Debi: *Schools rarely take a look at visual processing as it relates to children with learning difficulties. Why is this?*
Dr. Goedert: Understanding vision requires acceptance of a scholastic paradigm that is currently at odds with the mechanistic concept of the eye as a camera and the brain as a computer. Until learning is seen as the integration of sensory, emotional, and cognitive systems, the standard of care will remain the mechanist/ pharmaceutical approach.

Why do some children have a difficult time staying focused and motivated?

Margot traveled to Louisiana to talk with her good friend, Freddie Ann Regan, about behaviors we see in children having a difficult time focusing in the classroom environment. Freddie Ann is a physical therapist, with 24 years experience in Sensory Integration. She works with learning disabled and autistic children privately and in the school setting. In this interview she expands our knowledge of the role of the ANS and its relationship to classroom behavior, and offers valuable tips to maintaining positive behavior.

Freddie Ann: A child may have difficulty focusing, or appear hyperactive because he is experiencing difficulties at the autonomic nervous system level of the pyramid that you talked about in chapters 1 and 4. He may act out or be in a state of high frustration. The child may choose to "check out" altogether. Teachers often refer to this as staring into space or the "lights are on but no one is home" syndrome.

Margot: Why does a child experiencing difficulty at the ANS level act like this?
Freddie Ann: The child will communicate his needs through behavior rather than language. This provides strong communication for the child. A child's intelligence and his ability to communicate may not be a factor. The child has found it more effective to communicate by using behavior rather than using words.

Margot: What can a teacher do when he sees the ANS becoming involved in an inappropriate manner?
Freddie Ann: When a teacher learns to read the signs that the ANS is kicking in, he can intervene to change the environment the child is in. Learning to read signs of inappropriate arousal levels such as agitated movement, increased muscle tone, or lethargy can be an effective tool for teachers, and give them control over the situation with much less energy instead of putting out the fire after the fact.

Margot: You use the phrase, "Set them up for success." What do you mean by this?
Freddie Ann: A teacher can greatly increase the success children have in the classroom by observing body communication and behavior patterns. Teachers can choose the activity and then set the children's arousal level to be coherent with the activity. For

example, if I'm giving a lecture and I see people begin to slump in their chairs and yawn, I'll do an activity to increase their arousal level. I have them get up and "shake their booties," or do a quick activity to wake up the system. I do something from the outside to change things on the inside.

Margot: Can you elaborate on what you mean by "do something from the outside to change things on the inside."
Freddie Ann: Yes, children who are integrated can handle more input and adapt to the environment. Children with integration difficulties are not as adaptive to the situation. I call it, "having static in the system." It's like a radio that is not tuned right on the dial. There is a static signal coming in. This is very irritating and creates stress in the system. Observing and monitoring the ANS is the greatest tool a teacher has to increase peace and joy in the classroom. If the teacher can keep children balanced and off the stress mechanism, they will learn better. I call this "setting them up for success."

Margot: You refer to something called a "neurological fatigue break." What is this?
Freddie Ann: A neurological fatigue break is a chance for the children to fine tune their arousal level. If they are tired, they need movement to jazz up the system. If they are too wired for the activity, they need an opportunity to quiet themselves with deep breathing and soft music, for instance. This redirects the behavior before it becomes unmanageable. As an example, when children become antsy, I do an arousal dampening activity like deep pressure stimulation. The children compress their palms together, push their hands into the desk, and their feet into the floor to calm down the arousal level.

Margot: Can you give an example of how a teacher could provide the appropriate arousal level in the classroom?
Freddie Ann: The time of day can affect how the body is registering incoming information. For instance, in the morning when there needs to be a lot of listening and focus, a classroom that has full spectrum lighting, a moderate temperature, and a calming mood will generate the appropriate response from students. After lunch, teachers and children tend to be sleepy or lethargic. Providing activities calling for movement instead of listening and focus would be an appropriate arousal tool.

The specialists interviewed offer promising approaches for children with learning difficulties—many that could be remedied with appropriate therapy. Perhaps in the future, options such as vision and listening therapy will be an integral part of school services and not a fringe benefit, available only to children from families with the financial means to seek out and provide their children with the best treatments available. Our hope is for all children to reach their maximum learning potential, regardless of economic background. We have witnessed impressive growth in children who have been fortunate enough to receive services from the specialists we interviewed.

The following words of wisdom were printed in *The Learning Revolution* with credit given to Chen Jingpan, author of *Confucius as a Teacher*. These words remind us that there is much to relearn from the past. Blending the past with the exciting new methods available today will enhance learning for all children.

As Confucius said 2,500 years ago:

- *Blend the best of the new with the best from the old.*
- *Learn by doing.*
- *Use the world as classroom.*
- *Use music and poetry to learn and teach.*
- *Blend academic with physical.*
- *Learn how to learn, not just facts.*
- *Cater to different learning styles.*
- *Build good values and behavior.*
- *Provide an equal chance for all.*

"The final lesson of plasticity is that a human brain, given good foundations, can continue to adapt and expand for a lifetime...A well-nourished mind, well-grounded in the precursors of wisdom as well as of knowledge, will continue to grow, learn, develop–as long as it responds to the prickling of curiosity. Perhaps this quality, above all, is the one we should strive to preserve in all our children."

Jane M. Healy, Ph.D.
Endangered Minds

Chapter 12

Conclusion: Some Final Thoughts

- Ashley's Story
- Building a Solid Learning Foundation at Home and School

Ashley's Story

Would any book be complete if a wonderful story did not find itself somewhere in the final pages? We have many wonderful stories that we could share regarding the changes that take place while children are participating in S'cool Moves for Learning. One story stands out from the others. For privacy reasons we have changed the name of the little girl in the story.

Ashley began the program as a shy, withdrawn, and uncoordinated first grade student struggling academically and socially. She was having substantial difficulties at all levels of the Learning Pyramid. Her teacher was concerned at her lack of academic progress and social skills. Debi Heiberger, the reading specialist, met with Ashley and her mother to discuss the S'cool Moves for Learning program. Ashley's mother was enthusiastic about starting the program and offered to work with her daughter at home to compliment the school program.

Ashley was asked to draw a self-portrait of herself at the beginning of the program. The self-portrait was scanned at its actual size. The figure was small and missing limbs. Ashley used minimal space on the paper. The drawing indicated that Ashley had body image difficulties and lacked confidence.

Two months later, Ashley drew another self-portrait. The portrait had changed dramatically as she discovered how to comfortably move her body. The second drawing indicates improved body awareness. She drew herself with arms, hands, legs, and feet.

Notice the "X" crossing drawn in the dress, an indication that Ashley is discovering the midline of her body and becoming integrated. The face radiates joy, and the portrait has movement and flow.

Ashley participated in an individual S'cool Moves for Learning program in first grade and joined a small group program two days a week in fourth and fifth grade. Academically, Ashley made substantial improvement while she participated in the program, moving from the first stanine to the fourth stanine on standardized tests.[1] She maintained her gain through sixth grade, without the program.

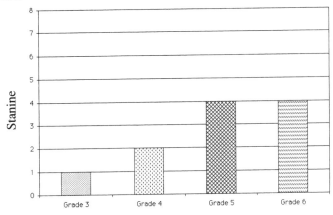

When Ashley's growth is compared to other students receiving supplemental academic services but not participating in the S'cool Moves for Learning program, she made the most consistent growth out of nine students in the group during four school years. Students A, C, E, and F did not have scores for some years because they moved and then relocated into the district.

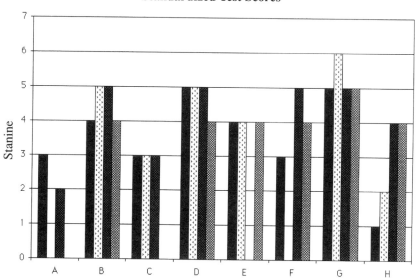

Standardized Test Scores

During a musical production, teachers commented that Ashley was the child who stood out from the other fifth grade students because of her ability to move her body with the music and truly enjoy herself on stage. Currently in junior high school, Ashley plays a musical instrument in the band, sings in the choir, and participates in cheerleading, volleyball, and basketball. She holds herself with a wonderful posture that shows confidence and poise. She works hard academically and meets her challenges head on.

We share this story to illustrate the changes that take place when a child's underlying difficulties are remedied. Children begin to experience life more fully. Quiet, reserved children become more animated and social; children afraid to take risks begin to venture out of their safety zones. Observable, wonderful changes begin to occur, often difficult to statistically measure.

Anecdotal and objective records provide evidence of positive outcome for children participating in S'cool Moves for Learning. Anecdotal records show children make gains in self esteem, confidence, social acceptance, and risk-taking. Self-portraits, writing samples, fluency statistics, and standardized tests measure change over time (see appendix A).

The example below shows the improvement in a fourth grade student's writing after doing a mixture of Cross Crawls, Squiggles, Paper Crumpling, and Figure 8's a few minutes every day for several weeks. Both writing samples were done in the same amount of time.

Before

> Sneakers
> I think that thay calld
> Jelly sneak and the shac
> ers and thay ᵃᵈᵈⁱⁿᵍ
> dropt. Some Jely in.

After

> School
> I like school. it is very fun.
> I have a lat of frends.
> I like to play with my
> frends. I like tittle one;
> it is a lot of fun; I wish
> I cood come to tittle
> one evry day. I like
> to read I can read for
> a long time I like to
> read it is fun.

Sometimes children need the entire program for dramatic changes to occur. Other times, a few simple movement activities make the right connections to remedy a problem. The bottom line is that integrative movement keep children in a positive learning state, making change and growth possible.

Building a Solid Learning Foundation at Home and School

There is a trend in education to standardize childrens' learning and expect all children to achieve high academic goals at specific grade levels. We must keep in mind that the normal developmental timelines cannot be neatly classified into grade levels.

Despite our fast-paced, technological era, children have their own developmental timelines. Pushing children into academics before they have developed a firm foundation, may, in the end, produce children who are burned out and unmotivated. This defeats the ultimate goal of becoming joyful, lifelong learners. If children become too stressed trying to fulfill academic expectations for which they are not ready, they may shut down.

S'cool Moves for Learning reduces the child's reaction to stress and creates pathways for enhanced communication within the body-mind system, but the movements cannot totally alleviate the stress a child may experience when asked to accomplish developmentally inappropriate tasks.

Schools that incorporate the IMAS, integrative movement programs, excellent reading instruction, and regard the importance of the emotional-heart connection will be leaders in education—like the school in Northern California where the statistical information was gathered. Their teachers and paraeducators are life-long learners expecting the best from themselves and their students—and getting it! This school serves as a model for what can be accomplished in today's educational system.

We conclude with a summary of ideas to help children build a solid learning foundation that will lead to positive learning experiences at home and school.

At home:
- During pregnancy, keep stress levels to a minimum. Take time out each day for deep breathing and relaxation. Your baby is aware of your feelings and responds to the chemicals in your system during extended periods of stress.

- Create a safe and loving home for your baby to play and learn. Give lots of hugs and kisses.
- Learn newborn and infant massage—treating you and your baby to a wonderful experience.
- Give babies lots of time on their bellies so they can flex and extend their bodies, roll over, belly crawl, and creep on hands and knees. Add encouragement along the way.
- Reduce the time babies spend in infant seats, bouncer seats, jumper seats, walkers, and playpens. Overuse of these items may interfere with the developmental process.
- Provide opportunities for toddlers to run, jump, skip, tumble, and roll.
- Reduce television viewing and computer usage. Instead, encourage imaginative play with family and friends. Television should be viewed from a distance of at least six feet away.
- Honor your child's unique developmental timeline and resist the temptation to compare your child with other children who may be developing faster or slower than your own child. There is a large window of normal development among typical, healthy children.
- Recapture the good ol' days by playing jacks, hopscotch, or pickup sticks with your child. Remember, "All work and no play makes for a very dull day," for children and adults alike.
- Encourage children to drink lots of water throughout the day. Soda and juices don't count. You wouldn't wash dishes in soda or juice. The same principle applies to using water to cleanse and nourish the body.

At school:
- Allow children time to explore, create, sing, and move freely.
- Encourage schools to adopt or keep programs that include art, music, and movement opportunities.
- If a child is ready for traditional academic learning, do so in a developmentally appropriate way: larger print for reading to assist eye muscles not yet developed for smaller print, larger writing tools until fine motor skills are in place, and writing at arms length on large paper until all the postural, balance, and kinesthetic skills are integrated.
- Allow children to take water breaks. The 3 sip rule works well. Each child takes 3 sips and sits back down. Some research is linking water bottles to increased illness due to

S'cool Moves for Learning

the lack of careful washing on a regular basis, and the children putting their hands on the spouts to pop them open after they have been exposed to potential germs from other children's hands, doorknobs, or school tools.
- Give positive feedback to school personnel who create a learning environment that supports all learners along the developmental spectrum.
- If other teachers are not familiar with the concepts in this book, share this information with them.
- Consider implementing a developmental assessment, such as the Integrated Motor Activity Screening. When children enter kindergarten, take time to meet with their parents or guardians to discuss their uterine, birth, and developmental histories, if appropriate.

We honor the multi-dimensional talents of people who work with children. We need a wide variety of approaches to meet the diverse needs of all children. *The Everyday Genius* written by Peter Kline describes a technique called Integrative Learning. He shares a story in his book about how a teacher turned a class of unmotivated, learning challenged students into enthusiastic, happy learners by using an Integrative Learning technique. He writes, "That was all it took—involvement of their bodies in the learning process—and they came to life. We didn't solve everything, but in a few moments we got a process going that can change learning behavior significantly and, perhaps, permanently."

S'cool Moves for Learning is a program that stands on its own, or can be blended with other successful methodologies, such as Integrative Learning. Together we can accomplish so much more than working alone. There is universal wisdom that fills all of us with the knowledge and intuition needed to nurture children. We must also provide one another with encouragement and support so we may continue to grow in love for our life's work, or perhaps we should say, "Our life's play."

Enjoy moving with your students, and remember to have at least one hearty laugh a day. The word "school" means leisure or pastime, because people felt that a boy was lucky to be in school, otherwise he'd be out in his father's shop, working in the fields, or milking cows.[2] That was real work and "school" was play. And as it should be today—playful, joyful learning.

S'cool Moves for Learning

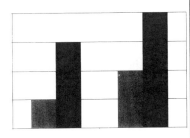

Appendix A

Statistical Data, 1995–2000

- School Demographics
- Program Design
- School Improvement Program (SIP)
- Title I
- The Integrated Motor Activities Screening (IMAS)

Statistical Data, 1995–2000

The following information was gathered as part of state and federal compliance requirements holding schools accountable for showing student progress toward meeting predetermined goals. This information was presented to School Board and Site Council Members as part of the annual review of state and federal programs targeting low achieving students. The two programs discussed are the School Improvement Program and Title I.

School Demographics

The school where this data was collected is located in a rural area of Northern California. The total population of K-8 students is approximately 470 students. The ethnic backgrounds are predominantly White. There is a small population of combined Native American, Hispanic, and Black students. The number of students receiving free or reduced lunches has risen in the last five years from 46.8% in 1995–1996 to 53% in 1999–2000. The daily absentee rate is substantially higher than the state average. The mobility rate is high among students receiving Title I and Special Education services.

Program Design

As part of the early intervention model, kindergarten and first grade students were screened with the *Integrated Motor Activities Screening* (IMAS) to ensure their learning foundations were solidly in place. Children who scored low or below average on the screening were targeted to participate in the S'cool Moves for Learning program working individually, or in small groups, with the reading specialist or specially trained paraeducators. The reading specialist assisted in designing individual programs for targeted students, and modeled S'cool Moves for Learning activities for primary teachers in their classrooms.

Students in first grade were assessed for reading ability using Marie Clay's *Observation Survey* and *Record of Oral Language*. The students' scores on the IMAS, *Observation Survey* and *Record of Oral Language* were used to determine placement in Reading Recovery and the Primary Reading Enrichment Program (PREP). First and second grade students scoring in the lowest quarter were supported through the services of a Miller-Unruh Reading

Recovery Teacher and a trained paraeducator. The students most prepared, based on the three measures, were chosen to enter the program the first quarter while the other students were provided with activities to improve their scores on the IMAS and *Record of Oral Language* and served the second, third, or fourth quarters of the year.

Students in third, fourth, and fifth grades were assessed using *Curriculum-Based Measurement* (CBM), reading inventories, or a modified IMAS. CBM is a way to measure student progress using actual passages from their reading curriculum. The lowest performing students received Title I services from the Title I Reading Specialist, or trained para-educator. Services included reading instruction and participation in S'cool Moves for Learning.

All primary teachers received specialized training in reading instruction and most were trained in using integrative movement with students in the classroom.

School Improvement Program (SIP)

The School Improvement Program's goal is to ensure that all students are meeting the high performance standards adopted at each grade level. The money received through this program is used to improve learning for all students and not specifically targeted to any particular group of students. To evaluate progress for all students, specific assessments were in place at each grade level. Primary, middle, and upper grades have a variety of benchmarks to ensure all students are making progress. Standardized testing, CBM, and fourth and seventh grade assessments have been used for the last five years to evaluate how well students were doing throughout the school and to compare growth from year to year.

All students participated in annual spring standardized testing except those exempted due to parent waiver, Individual Educational Program (IEP) modifications, or extended absences.

To analyze schoolwide fluency rates, students in grades 3-6 were assessed using CBM reading passages in fall of each school year. A median score was recorded each year with the goal of bringing Title I and Special Education students to the median of their classes. All students in fourth grade were given a grade level reading inventory each year to determine their percent accuracy and self correction rates. Students in seventh grade took proficiency tests in reading and math. The data collected on standardized test scores, CBM, and reading inventories determined the effectiveness of SIP. The standardized test scores for all students were analyzed by comparing growth from Spring 1996 to Spring 1999. The number of students who scored at or above the 50 percentile on the total scores for reading and math was recorded. The total scores included all subtests in reading and math. Scores for the 1999–2000 school year became available shortly before going to press and were included for further analysis of growth.

The Percentage of Students Scoring At or Above the 50 Percentile in Reading and Math from Spring 1996 to Spring 1999 Comparison of growth from Spring 1999 to Spring 2000

	Spring 1996	Spring 1999	Spring 2000
Reading	45.1	55.8	61.4
Math	38.2	59.8	67.3

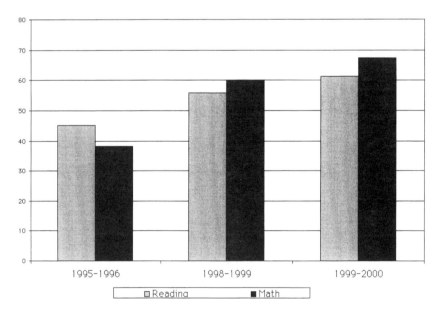

There has been substantial improvement in the percentage of students scoring at or above the 50 percentile from 1995–2000. The number of students at or above the 50 percentile has grown by 16.3% in reading and 29.1% in math.

S'cool Moves for Learning

Approximately 480 Title I students have been served between the years 1995–2000. This school qualified to apply for the national and state *Achieving Title I Schools Award* based on increased student achievement in reading and math in 1998–1999.

Curriculum-Based Measurement was used to record student fluency rates (words per minute) from 1995–1999 for students in grades 3 through 6. Fall median fluency rates have risen at each grade level.

Curriculum-Based Measurement Median Scores for Fourth, Fifth, and Sixth Grade Students

	Fall 1995	Fall 1998	Fall 1999
3rd	33	53	70
4th	51	69	95
5th	92	97	100
6th	no score	98	120

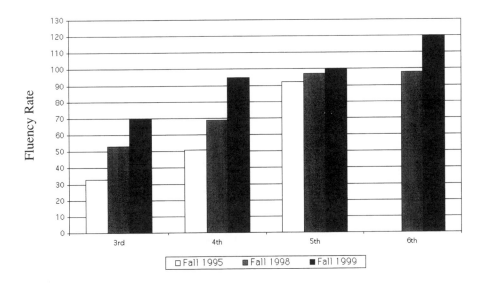

Title I

In fall 1999 fourth and sixth grade students receiving Title I services any time during their school careers were assessed using standardized reading passages and Curriculum-Based Measurement. The forty students were evaluated on their ability to read passages independently at 95% accuracy or better with a self-correction rate of at least 1:3. Students were also given a CBM reading passage to determine fluency based on a word per minute analysis.

All fourth and sixth grade students, including the Title I students, were able to read the passages independently (95%) or better. All but 5 students read at or above the median fluency rate for their grade level. Students receiving Special Education services are not included in this summary.

Number of Title I Students Tested	40
Fourth Grade	20
Sixth Grade	20
Percent Reading at Grade Level	100%

Fluency rates for fourth grade Title I students from mid-September to mid-December of the 1999–2000 school year were recorded to monitor growth during the first trimester and provide a "snapshot" of growth during a short period of time. The 13 students all made gains in three months time. The students participated in S'cool Moves for Learning while receiving reading services.

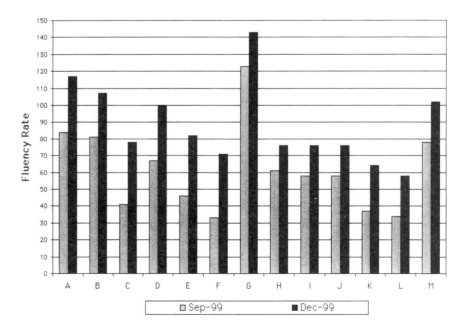

The Integrated Motor Activities Screening (IMAS)

S'cool Moves for Learning helped children improve their scores on the IMAS during the 1999–2000 school year. The kindergarten teachers used activities from the program daily with all their students. To determine how well the movement activities improved IMAS scores, a group of kindergarten students were screened with the IMAS in fall and spring of the same school year.

In fall, the kindergarten group had a high number of students performing in the low and below average ranges and few students scoring in the average to high ranges. In spring, fewer students scored in the low and below average ranges and most scored in the average to high ranges. The graph below illustrates the changes in student performance on the IMAS between fall and spring.

IMAS Fall and Spring Scores

The data on the next pages show pre and post IMAS assessment results for the kindergarten group in two classes and a K–1 combination class. The total number of students involved in the screening was 37. The graphs on pages 153–156 summarize student progress in the two kindergarten classes. Summary graphs are not included for students in the K–1 combination class.

Kindergarten Students' Scores on the IMAS for Fall and Spring

	Fall	Spring
High	1	8
Above Average	1	11
Average	6	6
Below Average	19	10
Low	10	2
Total Students	37	37

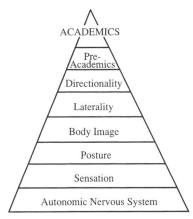

The Learning Pyramid

The reading specialist modeled S'cool Moves for Learning activities once a week in the kindergarten classrooms. Minute Moves were added to the regular classroom activities and to physical education periods. The teachers incorporated movements into the day, working with students at the laterality level of the pyramid. Some students needed focused participation at the lower levels of the Learning Pyramid, including sensation and posture. A paraeducator worked individually with students as the need arose.

Students performing in the below average or low range in spring were targeted to participate in an individually designed S'cool Moves for Learning program in first grade, or in a home program over the summer.

The charts on the remaining pages graphically represent fall and spring scores on the auditory-visual-motor, eye-hand coordination, and gross motor sections of the IMAS for students in the two kindergarten classes. Each class has a chart showing the total score performances for students in fall and spring. The K–1 combination class is not included in the graphed section due to the small sampling of kindergarten students. Fall scores are represented in each chart by bars with a white background. Spring scores are represented by bars with a dark background.

Appendix B discusses in greater detail how to successfully integrate the IMAS into a reading intervention program. Using the IMAS in conjunction with other measures, such as reading and language assessments, provides a holistic view of the child. The information gathered can be used to design a program for each child specifically tailored to meet individual needs.

S'cool Moves for Learning

Class 1 IMAS Auditory-Visual-Motor

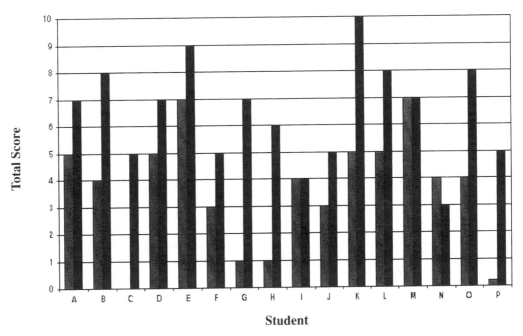

Class 1 IMAS Eye-Hand Coordination

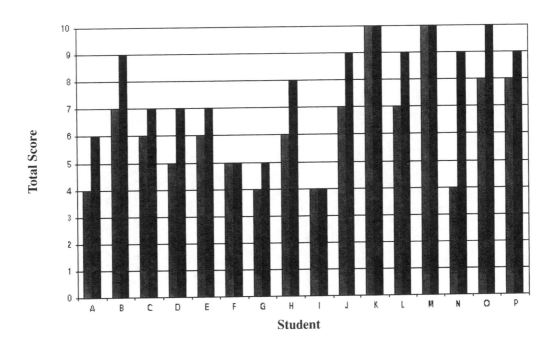

S'cool Moves for Learning

Class 1   IMAS Gross Motor

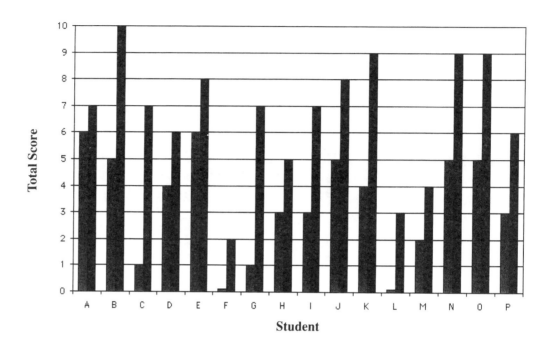

Class 1   IMAS Total Score

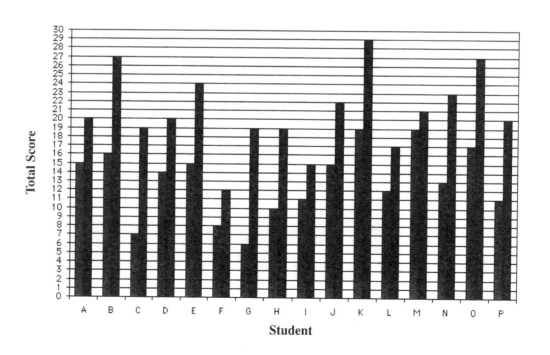

Class 2   IMAS Auditory-Visual-Motor

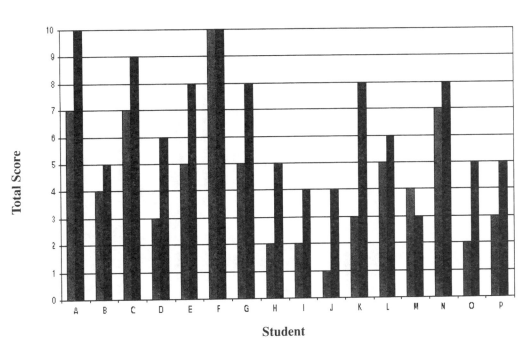

Class 2   IMAS Eye-Hand Coordination

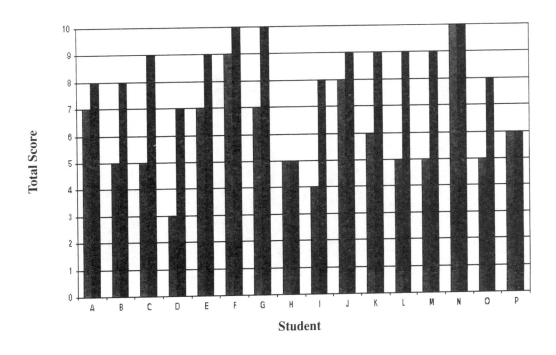

S'cool Moves for Learning

Class 2   IMAS Gross Motor

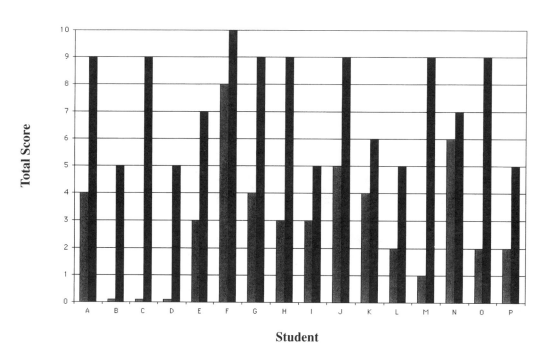

Class 2   IMAS Total Score

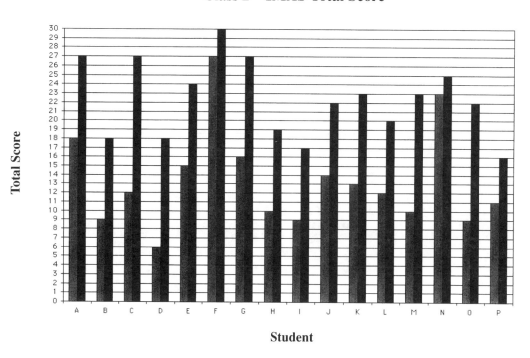

S'cool Moves for Learning

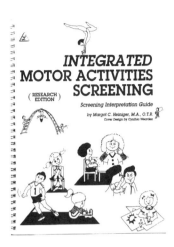

Appendix B

The Integrated Motor Activities Screening (IMAS)

- Using the IMAS to Compliment Reading Programs
- IMAS Student Data Summary Chart
- Relationship of IMAS Items to the Learning Pyramid
- IMAS Assessment Items and Classroom Implications

The Integrated Motor Activities Screening (IMAS)

Using the IMAS to Compliment Reading Programs

Based on the growing evidence validating integrative movement to improve learning potential, Title I students in grades three through five were selected to participate in a movement program to help with learning difficulties. All students qualified for the program through federally funded sources or the Resource Specialist Program (Special Education). While participating in the movement program, students began showing positive academic gains, improved behavior, and increased physical stamina and coordination. The elementary school staff chose to use the *Integrated Motor Activities Screening* (IMAS), developed by Margot Heiniger to screen kindergarten and first grade children providing earlier intervention for students with low scores and academic challenges.

The IMAS has proven to be a valuable piece of information in helping to determine the most powerful support to provide the low-progress student. When used in conjunction with S'cool Moves for Learning, Marie Clay's *Observation Survey* and *Record of Oral Language*, the IMAS was found to be a pivotal piece of the reading intervention program. Students were chosen for reading intervention according to their scores on all three measures. The most prepared students entered Reading Recovery the first quarter of the year, while the least prepared were involved in S'cool Moves for Learning and language acquisition activities.

Using the three measures made it possible to look at key pieces that create a strong learning foundation in young children: developmental skills, language acquisition, and reading skills. By taking into account how children perform on all three measures, a holistic profile of the child emerges.

When children began intensive reading instruction with their scores on the IMAS and *Record of Oral Language* in the average or higher ranges they were able to learn with less stress and progress more quickly.

Children older than the IMAS norming group (4–6.5 years of age), were assessed with the IMAS as part of the Title I program, but modifications were made to the eye-hand coordination screening items. In place of the coloring activities, samples of children's writing were collected and evaluated. In addition, children were asked to reproduce the geometric forms shown below. The numbers above the figures represent the approximate age when a child is able to duplicate the drawings.[1]

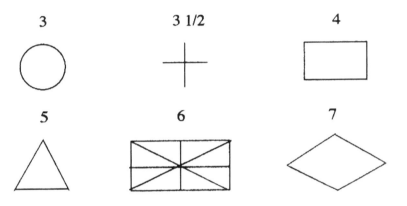

Below is an example of a child's drawing indicating difficulty crossing the midline of the body. Each crossing line is drawn as a separate line.

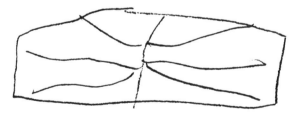

Circles should be drawn counter-clockwise for a right-handed child and clockwise for a left-handed child. Reversals in these patterns suggest midline difficulties.

Young children were also asked to draw pictures of themselves to show body image and their sense of spatial relationships.

What about the children who do well academically but score poorly on the IMAS? We recommend these children be monitored closely to ensure that they do not work harder than other children to accomplish the same level of competency. If so, that energy could be used to further their academic talents. For example, some children score in the average range on reading assessments at the start of the year, and score low on the IMAS. Often, the students don't hold onto their average standing as the year progresses. They drop to the low portion of the class and need more reading support. Teachers will comment that they have students who start the year off with lots of energy and make good progress but lose ground as the year goes on. The reading specialist noticed that she could move her students further in less time when their IMAS scores were average or higher.

The IMAS consists of two sections. One section is recorded observations and the other is scored. If a child has difficulty with any of the screening items, there may be classroom implications (discussed briefly in the remainder of this chapter).

Observation Sections
- Eye Control
- Dominance
- Body Awareness
- Posture and Muscle Tone
- Behavior Patterns

Scored Sections
- Auditory-Visual-Motor
- Eye-Hand Coordination
- Gross Motor

The following pages include two charts. The first chart may be used to record student scores on the IMAS. The second chart—Relationship of IMAS Items to the Learning Pyramid—may be used to determine where to start a child in the program. To use the chart, look for the screening item that the child had difficulty with and follow across the chart to the marked section that correlates with the chapters in this book. For instance if a child is experiencing posture difficulties, start the child with the movements in the sensation or posture chapters.

IMAS Student Data Summary Chart

Teacher: _____ Date: _____

Student Name	Eye Control	Dominance	Body Awareness	Posture	Behavior	Auditory-Visual-Motor	Eye-Hand	Gross Motor	Total Score

Relationship of IMAS Items to the Learning Pyramid

Integrated Motor Activity Screening (IMAS) Item	ANS	Sensation	Posture	Body Image	Laterality	Directionality	Pre-Academics (A-V Motor)
Eye Control	x	x	x		x	x	x
Dominance			x		x	x	x
Body Awareness		x		x			x
Posture and Muscle Tone		x	x		x		
Behavior Patterns	x	x	x	x	x	x	x
Auditory-Visual-Motor	x	x	x		x	x	x
Eye-Hand Coordination	x	x	x		x	x	x
Gross Motor: Balancing on one foot		x	x		x	x	x
Hopping on each foot		x	x		x	x	x
Skipping		x	x		x	x	x
Tossing a ball		x	x		x	x	x
Catching a ball		x	x		x	x	x
Tossing in air and catching a ball (to self)		x	x		x	x	x
Difficulties with all items	x	x	x	x	x	x	x

IMAS Assessment Items and Classroom Implications

Eye Control: Monocular, Binocular, and Convergence

- difficulty following a line of text while reading, or may skip letters and/or words while reading
- difficulty adding numbers in a column
- difficulty copying from the board to paper
- poor writing quality
- difficulty with spatial relationships
- difficulty with spelling
- poor depth perception
- frustrated during many fine and gross motor tasks

Dominance: Eye, Hand, and Foot

- lack of a dominant hand will make fine motor tasks difficult
- left eye dominance could cause reading difficulties and letter or number reversal
- mixed dominance may be a sign of laterality difficulties
- eye dominance that is opposite of hand dominance may make writing and fine motor tasks difficult

Body Awareness

- holds onto other children
- runs a hand along the wall while walking
- frequently bumps into others
- slow to respond to auditory commands when asked to point to body parts may indicate problems with taking in auditory information efficiently, or a delay in processing due to hearing difficulties

Posture

- fatigues easily and may not finish work
- handwriting becomes more difficult to read from the start to end of the assignment
- awkwardness and lack of coordination during physical education and playground activities
- sideliners—while standing and watching other children play
- may constantly change position to rest muscles (giving the appearance of hyperactivity)
- classroom interaction and success is limited by the need to focus on the body

- rarely have the correct book, page, worksheet, or materials for an activity
- very disruptive in the classroom—constant movement and interruptions
- short attention span
- trouble getting along with others
- frequently falls, stumbles, or bumps into things
- concentration is limited because energy is being expended to maintain balance
- difficulty filtering out background noise and visual distraction.

Behavior

- potential for being labeled as having Attention Deficit Hyperactivity Disorder since they have difficulty working alone or are distracted by noises in the classroom, hall, or outside the building
- distracted by visual stimuli such as pictures and decorations on a bulletin board, as well as the flicker and buzz of fluorescent lights
- when feeling inadequate, may use the excuse that the work is too easy, or call it "baby stuff"
- potential class clowns who attempt to control the teacher and classroom situation to conform to their activities instead of adhering to the classroom schedule

Auditory-Visual-Motor

- needs additional time to process information
- may need to repeat an activity many times before it becomes automatic
- writing, drawing, pasting, and coloring activities may be difficult
- rhythm games and playground activities may be difficult
- constantly talking without allowing others to speak
- may draw or write the same things over and over
- difficulty following directions, responding to visual and auditory clues, discriminating sounds, associating and sequencing stimuli
- letter or number reversal
- slow to start working or looks around to see what the other children are doing before getting started

Eye-Hand Coordination
- difficulty handling crayons, scissors, pencils, and completing fine motor tasks
- difficulty performing finger plays
- poor self-help skills requiring fine motor control
- avoidance or dislike of fine motor activities
- inappropriate pencil grip or pencil pressure; poor organization and legibility during writing activities
- uncoordinated in physical education and activities requiring eye-hand skill such as throwing, catching, and hitting a ball

Gross Motor Skills
- may be clumsy, bump into furniture, stumble, or fall frequently
- lacks coordination during physical education and playground games requiring flexibility, balance, and timing
- fine motor skills develop out of gross motor skills, therefore fine motor skills may be affected
- short attention span due to balance problems
- difficulty with activities requiring timing and rhythm
- expends a lot of energy to get academic work done due to needing to focus on gross motor skills such as balance and fine motor coordination

Margot's One Minute Assessment
If Margot had one minute to assess a student, she would have the child balance on one leg with her eyes open and then closed, self-toss a ball in the air and catch it, and snap her fingers. These items would tell her a lot about how the child has integrated the elements of the Learning Pyramid.

Appendix C

Margot Heiniger and Shirley Randolph's Work

- The Tree of Learning
- The Pyramid of Learning

The Tree of Learning

Neurophysiological Concepts in Human Behavior, co-authored by Margot Heiniger and Shirley Randolph is no longer in print. Due to the difficulty in obtaining the book, the original work is included here for easy reference.

"The tree is a model of the individual. The ground depicts the autonomic nervous system, which influences how all information is interpreted. Each root of the tree represents a different source of sensory information. The sensory information must travel up to higher levels of the nervous system, depicted by the branches of the tree, to be integrated and available for motor expression."

Quote and Ilustration from Heiniger, Margot C. and Randolph, Shirley L. 1985. *Neurophysiological Concepts in Human Behavior.* Boise: The Tree of Learning Press.

The Pyramid of Learning

The Learning Pyramid used in this book was modified from the original Pyramid of Learning, mentioned in chapter 1.

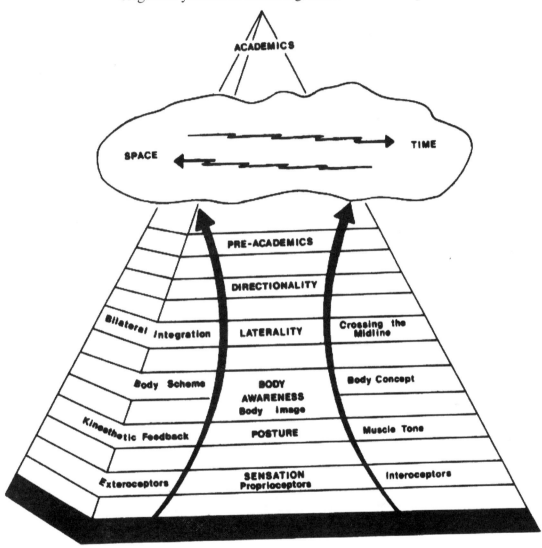

The pyramid is a model of the developmental sequence of education. We marvel at our failure to realize what is so obvious—that learning is a total mind, body, and spirit experience. Learning in any area, physical, emotional, intellectual, or spiritual, involves the whole person. Anyone in a helping profession must be cognizant of the interdependence of all areas and all professions."

Quote and Ilustration from Heiniger, Margot C. and Randolph, Shirley L. 1985. *Neurophysiological Concepts in Human Behavior.* Boise: The Tree of Learning Press.

Chapter Reference Notes

Chapter 1 The Integrated Learner
1. Personal communication with Dr. Bruce Lipton.
2. Randolph, Shirley L., and Heiniger, Margot C. 1998. *Kids Learn From the Inside Out: How to Enhance the Human Matrix*. Boise: Legendary Publishing Company.
3. Learning Magazine May/June 1996, p.43.
4. Cohen, Bonnie Bainbridge. 1993. *Sensing, Feeling, and Action*. Northampton: Contact Editions.
5. Pert, Candace B. 1999. *Molecules of Emotion*. New York: Touchstone, New York.
6. Heiniger, Margot C., and Randolph, Shirley L. 1985. *Neurophysiological Concepts in Human Behavior*. Boise: The Tree of Learning Press.
7. Randolph, Shirley L, and Heiniger, Margot C. 1998. *Kids Learn From the Inside Out: How to Enhance the Human Matrix*. Boise: Legendary Publishing Company.
8. Heiniger, Margot C., and Randolph, Shirley L. 1985. *Neurophysiological Concepts in Human Behavior*. Boise: The Tree of Learning Press.
9. Williams, Mary Sue, and Shellenberger, Sherry. 1996. "How Does Your Engine Run?" Albuquerque: TherapyWorks, Inc.
10. Sylwester, Robert. 1995. *A Celebration of Neurons*. Alexandria: Association of Supervision and Curriculum Development.
11. Dryden, Gordon and Vos, Jeannette. 1999. *The Learning Revolution*. Torrance: The Learning Web. Permission granted to reprint chart.
12. Dryden, Gordon and Vos, Jeannette. 1999. *The Learning Revolution*. Torrance: The Learning Web.
13. Kephart, Newell C. 1971. *The Slow Learner in the Classroom*. Columbus: Charles E. Merrill.
14. Sylwester, Robert. 1995. *A Celebration of Neurons*. Alexandria: Association of Supervision and Curriculum Development.
15. Dennison, Paul E., and Dennison, Gail E. 1994. *Brain Gym®, Teacher's Edition*. Ventura: Educational Kinesiology Foundation.
16. Kephart, Newell C. 1971. *The Slow Learner in the Classroom*. Columbus: Charles E. Merrill.

17. Promislow, Sharon. 1999. *Making the Brain Body Connection*. West Vancourver B.C. Kinetic Publishing Corporation.
18. Sylwester, Robert. 1995. *A Celebration of Neurons*. Alexandria: Association of Supervision and Curriculum Development.
19. Hannaford, Carla. 1995. *Smart Moves: Why Learning Is Not All In Your Head*. Arlington: Great Ocean Publishers.
20. Dennison, Paul E., and Dennison, Gail E. 1994. *Brain Gym®, Teacher's Edition*. Ventura: Educational Kinesiology Foundation.
21. See www.interactivemetronome.com.
22. Pert, Candace B. 1999. *Molecules of Emotion*. New York: Touchstone, New York.
23. Sylwester, Robert. 1995. *A Celebration of Neurons*. Alexandria: Association of Supervision and Curriculum Development.
24. Hannaford, Carla. 1995. *Smart Moves: Why Learning Is Not All In Your Head*. Arlington: Great Ocean Publishers.
25. Dennison, Paul E., and Dennison, Gail E. 1994. *Brain Gym®, Teacher's Edition*. Ventura: Educational Kinesiology Foundation.

Chapter 2 S'cool Moves for Learning: An Overview
1. Freeman, Cecilia K. 1997. *I am the Child: Using Brain Gym® with Children Who Have Special Needs*. Ventura: Educational Kinesiology Foundation.

Chapter 4 Autonomic Nervous System
1. Jensen, Eric. 1996. *Brain-Based Learning*. Del Mar: Turning Point Publishing.
2. Movement modified from Hannaford, Carla. 1997. The Physiological Basis of Learning and Kinesiology (class).
3. Movement modified from Thie, John. 1994. Touch For Health (class).

Chapter 6 Posture
1. Source: American Chiropractic Association, 1701 Clarendon Blvd., Arlington, VA 22209. 800.986.4636.
2. Hickey, Mary C. August, 1999. *Mom, My Back Really Hurts*. Business Week. p. 115–116.

Chapter 8 Laterality
1. Movement modified from Davies, Elizabeth. 1989. *Perceptual-Motor Remedial Activities and Developmental P.E. Continuum*. Self-published.
2. Kephart, Newell C. 1971. *The Slow Learner in the Classroom*. Columbus: Charles E. Merrill.
3. Movement modified from Davies, Elizabeth. 1989. *Perceptual-Motor Remedial Activities and Developmental P.E. Continuum*. Self-published.

Chapter 9 Directionality
1. Hannaford, Carla. 1995. *Smart Moves: Why Learning Is Not All In Your Head*. Arlington: Great Ocean Publishers.
2. Kephart, Newell C. 1971. *The Slow Learner in the Classroom*. Columbus: Charles E. Merrill.

Chapter 10 Pre-Academics
1. Movement modified from Davies, Elizabeth. 1989. *Perceptual-Motor Remedial Activities and Developmental P.E. Continuum*. Self-published.

Chapter 11 Academics
1. Kephart, Newell C. 1971. *The Slow Learner in the Classroom*. Columbus: Charles E. Merrill.
2. Neill, Lee, and Brown, Jan. 1991. Preparing Children for Handwriting, *Sensory Integration Quarterly*, 4, p.1 and p. 3.
3. Promislow, Sharon. 1999. *Making the Brain Body Connection*. West Vancouver B.C.: Kinetic Publishing Corporation.

Chapter 12 Conclusion
1. Highet, Gilbert. 1950. *The Art of Teaching*. New York: Alfred A. Knopf, Inc.
2. A stanine is a statistical reference used when comparing standardized test scores from different publishers. Stanines 1, 2, and 3 represent below average ranges. Stanines 4, 5, and 6 represent average ranges. Stanines 7, 8, and 9 represent above average ranges.

Appendix B The Integrated Motor Activities Screening
1. DeBoer, Bob, et al. 1997. *A Chance to Learn Curriculum*. Minneapolis: A Chance to Grow, Inc.

Illustration Credits

Illustrations used in chapter 1

Randolph, Shirley L., and Heiniger, Margot C. 1998. *Kids Learn From the Inside Out: How to Enhance the Human Matrix.* Boise: Legendary Publishing Company.

Heiniger, Margot C., and Randolph, Shirley L. 1985. *Neurophysiological Concepts in Human Behavior.* Boise: The Tree of Learning Press.

References

Ayres, A. J. 2000. *Sensory Integration and the Child.* Los Angeles: Western Psychological Services.

Ballinger, Erich. 1996. *The Learning Gym.* Ventura: Educational Kinesiology Foundation.

Breggin, Peter. 1998. *Talking Back to Ritalin.* Monroe: Common Courage Press.

Chamberlain, David B. 1983. *Consciousness at Birth: A Review of the Emperical Evidence.* San Diego: Chamberlain Communications.

Chamberlain, David B. 1988. *Babies Remember Birth.* Los Angeles: Tarcher.

Cherry, Clare, Godwin, Douglas, and Staples, Jesse. 1989. *Is the Left Brain Always Right? A Guide to Whole Child Development.* Belmont: Fearon Teacher Aids.

Clay, Marie M. 1993. *An Observation Survey.* Aukland: Heinemann Education.

Clay, Marie M., et al. 1983. *Record of Oral Language and Biks and Gutches.* Aukland: Heinemann Education.

Cohen, Bonnie Bainbridge. 1993. *Sensing, Feeling, and Action.* Northampton: Contact Editions.

Davies, Elizabeth. 1989. *Perceptual-Motor Remedial Activities and Developmental P.E. Continuum.* Self-published.

DeBoer, Bob, et al. 1997. *A Chance to Learn Curriculum.* Minneapolis: A Chance to Grow, Inc.

Dennison, Paul E., and Dennison, Gail E. 1994. *Brain Gym®, Teacher's Edition.* Ventura: Educational Kinesiology Foundation.

Damasio, Antonio. *The Feeling of What Happens.* 1999. New York: Harcourt Brace & Company.

Dryden, Gordon and Vos, Jeannette. 1999. *The Learning Revolution.* Torrance: The Learning Web.

Educational Kinesiology Foundation. 1997. *Brain Gym® Handbook.* Ventura: Educational Kinesiology Foundation

Freeman, Cecilia K. 1997. *I am the Child: Using Brain Gym® with Children Who Have Special Needs.* Ventura: Educational Kinesiology Foundation.

Gesell, Arnold. 1940. *The First Five Years of Life.* New York: Harper & Row.

Goddard, Sally. 1995. *A Teacher's Window into a Child's Mind.* Eugene: Fern Ridge Press.

Gold, Svea. 1997. *If Kids Just Came With Instruction Sheets.* Eugene: Fern Ridge Press.

Grof, Stanislov. 1985. *Beyond the Brain: Birth, Death and Transcendence in Psychotherapy.* New York: State University of New York Press.

Hannaford, Carla. 2002. *Awakening the Child Heart.* Captain Cook: Jamilla Nur Publishing

Hannaford, Carla. 1997. *The Dominance Factor: How Knowing Your Dominant Eye, Ear, Brain, Hand & Foot Can Improve Your Learning.* Arlington: Great Ocean Publishers.

Hannaford, Carla. 1995. *Smart Moves: Why Learning Is Not All In Your Head.* Arlington: Great Ocean Publishers.

Harmon, Darrell Boyd. 1949. *The Coordinated Classroom.* Santa Ana: Optometric Extension Program Foundation, Inc.

Healy, Jane M. 1990. *Endangered Minds.* New York: Touchstone.

Heiberger, Debra Wilson and Heiniger-White, Margot. 2001. *Minute Moves for the Classroom.* Shasta: Integrated Learner Press.

Heiniger, Margot C. 1990. *The Integrated Motor Activities Screening.* Boise: Legendary Publishing Company.

Heiniger, Margot C., and Randolph, Shirley L. 1985. *Neurophysiological Concepts in Human Behavior.* Boise: The Tree of Learning Press. Out of print.

Hickey, Mary C. August, 1999. *Mom, My Back Really Hurts.* Business Week. p. 115-116.

Highet, Gilbert. 1950. *The Art of Teaching.* New York: Alfred A. Knopf, Inc.

Janov, Arthur. 1983. *Imprints: The Lifelong Effects of the Birth Experience.* New York: Coward-McCann.

Jensen, Eric. 1996. *Brain-Based Learning.* Del Mar: Turning Point Publishing.

Kaplan, Robert-Michael. 1994. *Seeing Without Glasses.* Oregon: Beyond Words Publishing, Inc.

Kephart, Newell C. 1971. *The Slow Learner in the Classroom.* Columbus: Charles E. Merrill. Out of print.

Klaus, Marshall H., and Kennell, John H. 1976. *Maternal-Infant Bonding.* Missouri: C.V. Mosby Company.

Klaus, Marshall H., and Klaus, Phyllis H. 1985. *The Amazing Newborn: Making the Most of the First Weeks of Life.* Boston: Addison-Wesley.

Kline, Peter. 1988. *The Everyday Genius.* Arlington: Great Ocean Publishers.

Kohn, Alfie. 1999. *The Schools Our Children Deserve.* New York: Houghton Mifflin Company.

Kranowitz, Carol Stock. 1998. *The Out-of-Sync Child.* New York: The Berkley Publishing Group.

Kuczen, Barbara. 1982. *Childhood Stress: Don't Let Your Child Be a Victim.* New York: Delacorte.

Lane, Kenneth A. 1993. *Developing Your Child For Success.* Lewisville: Learning Potentials Publishers, Inc.

Lipton, Bruce. 1999. Personal communication.

Madaule, Paul. 1994. *When Listening Comes Alive.* Norval: Moulin Publishing.

Magid, Ken, and McKelvey, Carole A. 1987. *High Risk: Children Without a Conscience.* New York: Paulist Prest.

Montagu, Ashley. 1978. *Touching: Human Significance of Skin.* New York: Harper and Row.

Neill, Lee, and Brown, Jan. 1991. Preparing Children for Handwriting, *Sensory Integration Quarterly*, 4, p.1 and p. 3.

Optometric Extension Program. 1994. *Vision Therapy: Training Laterality & Directionality.* Santa Ana: Optometric Extension Program.

Pearce, Joseph Chilton. 1992. *Magical Child.* New York: Bantam.

Pert, Candace B. 1999. *Molecules of Emotion.* New York: Touchstone, New York.

Promislow, Sharon. 1999. *Making the Brain Body Connection.* West Vancouver, B.C: Kinetic Publishing Corporation.

Randolph, Shirley L, and Heiniger, Margot C. 1998. *Kids Learn From the Inside Out: How to Enhance the Human Matrix.* Boise: Legendary Publishing Company.

Ridgeway, Roy. 1987. *The Unborn Child: How to Recognize and Overcome Prenatal Trauma.* Great Britain: Wildwood House.

Sunbeck, Deborah. 1996. *Infinity Walk: Preparing Your Mind to Learn.* Carson: Jalmar Press.

Shinn, M.R. 1989. *Curriculum-Based Measurement: Assessing Special Children.* New York: Guilford Press.

Sifft, Josie M. 1999. *Educational Kinesiology Foundation Research Report.* Ventura: Educational Kinesiology Foundation.

Sunbeck, Deborah. 1996. *Infinity Walk.* Torrance: Jalmar Press.

Sylwester, Robert. 1995. *A Celebration of Neurons.* Alexandria: Association of Supervision and Curriculum Development.

Thie, John. 1994. *Touch For Health.* Marina del Rey: DeVorss & Company.

Verny, Thomas, with Kelly, John. 1981. *The Secret Life of the Unborn Child.* New York: Dell.

Verny, Thomas R. 1987. *Pre- and Peri-Natal Psychology: An Introduction.* New York: Human Sciences Press, Inc.

Verny, Thomas, and Weintraub, Pamela. 1991. *Nurturing the Unborn Child.* New York: Delacorte.

Williams, Mary Sue, and Shellenberger, Sherry. 1996. *"How Does Your Engine Run?"* Albuquerque: TherapyWorks, Inc.

Zion, Leela C. 1994. *The Physical Side of Learning.* Byron: Front Row Experience.

For More Information

Bal-A-Vis-X
Bill Hubert
www.bal-a-vis-x.com, balavisx@mac.com
Rhythmic Balance/Auditory-Vision eXercises for Brain & Brain/Body Integration for elementary, middle, and high school students. Training video, book, and inservices available

Center for Communication & Learning Skills
Judith B. Belk, Ph.D., CCC-SLP/A
14674 SW Rainbow Drive, Lake Oswego, OR 97035
503.699.9022
Specializing in speech-language therapy programs, auditory and visually-based programs, and EEG Neurofeedback training

Developmental Delay Resources
www.devdelay.org, devdelay@mindspring.com
Newsletter and services regarding successful multi-disciplinary approaches for children with developmental delays

Educational Kinesiology Foundation
1691 Spinnaker Drive, Suite 105B, Ventura, CA 93001
805.658.7942 or 800.356.2109, www.braingym.org
For more information on Brain Gym® and related courses

Five Minutes to Better Reading Skills
Bonnie Terry Learning
www.bonnieterrylearning.com, btlearn@jps.net
(Visual tracking and phonetic word skills)

Cecilia K. Freeman, M.Ed.
www.iamthechild.com
Specializing in using Brain Gym® for children with special needs

Steven Goedert, O.D.
1225 Eureka Way, Ste. A, Redding, CA 96001
530.241.9650
Specializing in vision therapy and school inservices

Linda Howe, M.A.
4187 Bernardo Ct., Chino, CA 91710
909.628.9441
Perceptual-Motor consultant who trained with Elizabeth Davies

Stacey Neill, OTR, Sensory Integration Therapist
P.O. Box 991173, Redding, CA 96099
530.945.9571, StaceyOT4kids@aol.com

Optometric Extension Program 800.424.8070
(To order Marsden Balls and other vision training supplies)

READ KWIK:LEARN QUICK
Jerry L. Coker, Director
530.474.1196
(Breaking words into combinations and visual tracking activities)

Freddie Ann Regan, P.T.
611 W. College St., Lake Charles, LA 70605
318.477.8823
Specializing in Sensory Integration and Autism

Linda Michaels-Spivey, MS, CIMI
P.O. Box 680, Weaverville, CA 96093
530.524.2744, lindaspivey@excite.com
Certified Infant Massage Instructor and Neuro-Physical Integration Specialist

Laura Sobell, MA
www.calmbaby.com
For her book and video on how to calm high stress babies

STAR Foundation
Barbara Findeisen, MFT, President
888.857.7827, www.starfound.org
Margot Heiniger-White is currently on staff at STAR, a 10-day retreat empowering adults to resolve previously immovable developmental and psychological blocks

Stretchwell
www.stretchwell.com, 888.396.2430
(inexpensive gym balls and therapy balls)

Therapro, Inc.
225 Arlington Street
Framingham, MA 01702-8723
508.872.9494, 800.257.5376
(Education-related therapy materials, books, and useful items)

Toddler-Kindy GymbaROO Pty. Ltd.
142 Cotham Road, Kew, Cotham PO Box 3095
Kew, Victoria Australia 3101
(03) 9817 3544, office@gymbaroo.com.au
www.gymbaroo.com.au
Books, videos, and movement program for infants and toddlers

Ann Davies-White
559.784.6713, www.center4success.com
Elizabeth Davies' daughter, specializing in perceptual-motor development

Tapes and radio program produced by New Dimensions Foundation, 1.800.935.8273 or www.newdimensions.org.
Hannaford, Carla: Learning with Body and Mind, tape #2572
Lipton, Bruce and Findeisen, Barbara. Birth and Violence: The Social Impact, 1995.
Lipton, Bruce, Findeisen, Barbara, and Heiniger-White, Margot. Birthing, Biology, and Culture, 1997.

S'cool Moves for Learning

Music Selections

"Music reduces stress, relieves anxiety, increases energy, and improves recall. Music makes people smarter."
                Jeannette Vos
                The Music Revolution
                as quoted in *The Learning Revolution*

Rainbow Planet tapes and CD's
253.265.3758
E-mail: jimvalley@rainbowplanet.com
Website: www.rainbowplanet.com
Jim Valley offers Rainbow Planet Workshops to schools with the goal of enhancing children's learning through music, movement, and song writing.

Songs from the Rainbow Planet tape or CD to awaken, energize, and integrate children for learning are listed below.

Rainbow Planet: a fun, upbeat song with great words about getting along with one another. Cross Crawl, Rhythm Tapping, and any of the Figure 8 movements work well.

Bo-wo-wones: follow along with the music as the singer tells the students what movements to do. At the beginning, add Cross Crawls and make Figure 8's with the elbows and knees. Add Rhythm Tapping anywhere in the song. When the arms are up in the air, have the children do OK's to the music.

I Feel Proud: a great song to relieve test anxiety. Have the children sing the song while doing Cross Crawls, Figure 8's with the body, Partner 8's, Balance 8's, Air 8's, and Listening Ears. Let children choose movements they like while moving to the song.

The Computer Song: a fun song to sing with lots of oral motor expression ("cling," "clang," "bing," "bang," and other engaging sounds). All the movements work well with this song.

Splish Splash: from the oldies version with children singing the lyrics. Snap the fingers at the beginning of the song and then add the One Minute Warm-up for Writing. This song works well for improving sensation and the words lend themselves nicely, "rub dub just relaxing in the tub." Perform movements that go with the words and you can't go wrong!

Integrate literature by using the big books and student books to the songs Rainbow Planet and Bo-wo-wones. Have students make their own big books to the other songs.

Calming, integrating music from Enya's Paint the Sky With Stars tape or CD
Book of Days and Caribbean Blue: these songs have a beautiful flow and work well with Partner 8's and Drawing 8's at the desk. Shepherd Moons and Watermark have a beautiful musical score that lends itself to the Developmental Symphony I and Developmental Symphony II. Enya's music may be purchased through most music stores.

Celtic Nights by NorthSound tape or CD has a collection of beautiful songs with nature sounds blended (rain, water flowing, insect, animal, and bird sounds). The songs that work particularly well include Moon Dance for Cross Crawling slowly and more quickly and doing Minute Warm-ups for Reading and Writing;
Spring Faire has the perfect beat to use for Rhythm Tapping. This tape may be purchased through music stores, specialty nature stores, or National Park gift shops.

For children with specialized needs TherapyWorks produces a tape titled The Alert Program with Songs for Self-Regulation. The songs help children regulate their activity levels so they can learn better. This tape may be purchased from TherapyWorks or Therapro, listed in the For More Information section.

Index

A Teacher's Window Into the Child's Mind 1
academics
    alphabet 122
    incorporating movement 122–124
    Learning Pyramid overview 19
    and listening 128–129
    organization for 120–121
    and sensory integration 134–135
    strategies for success 121
    student profile 120
    and visual processing 130–133
    writing difficulties 127
Air 8's 92
All Fours Balance 69–70
alphabet 122
Angel Taps
    and body image 79
    and directionality 104
ANS-Survival level
    difficulties 134–135
    overview 45–51
    Learning Pyramid overview 12–14
    Minute Moves 50–51
    strategies for success 48–49
    student profile 47
arousal levels
    monitoring 12–14, 134–135,
    See also ANS-Survival level
Ashley's story 138–141
attention. *See* focus
auditory figure-ground 78
auditory skills
    overview 118
    See also listening
auditory system, integrating 36
auditory-motor activities 107
auditory-visual-motor skills
    activities 107, 111, 155, 164
    graph of scores 155
    IMAS assessment items 164
Autonomic Nervous System (ANS). *See* ANS-Survival level

back writing 101
backpacks 67
balance
    All Fours Balance 69–70
    Balance 8's 92
    Forearm Balance 68–69

        Half-Kneel Balance   71
        Knee Balance   71
        Rocking Balance 69
        Sitting Balance   71–72
        Standing Balance 72
        Sway Balance   72–73
        See also posture
Balance 8's   92
balance board   123
Ball-Games   89–91
basic extension   59–60
behavior, graph of scores   153
behavior, IMAS assessment items   164
Belk, Judith
        consultation   5
        interview   128–129
        contact information   178
belly crawling   4, 66
Body 8's   80
body awareness, IMAS assessment items   163
body image
        Angel Taps   79
        Body 8's   80
        chart of behavior 76
        Learning Pyramid overview   17
        overview   75–82
        self-portraits   31, 80, 138–139, 159
        strategies for success   78
        student profile   77
bonding 23
boundaries activities   78
Brain Gym   178
breathing, deep   50
butterfly extension   60
Butterfly Legs   58–59
Butterfly Wings   58

carpet square activities
        boundaries   78
        directionality   104
        laterality   95–97
case studies. *See* student profiles
catching activities   118
Center for Communication & Learning Skills   178
Certificate of Participation 42
chart of behavior
        body image   76
        directionality   100
        laterality   84
        posture   64
        sensation   54

Chart of Behavior 6–10
Clapping-Tapping Game 112
classroom desk placement 78, 103, 126
classroom lighting 131–132
Clay, Marie 146, 158
Clock Game 104
Cocoons 57–58
Cohen, Bonnie Bainbridge xii, 12, 25
compensating behavior 34–36
Cross Crawl Robo-Pats 89
Cross Crawls
    and ANS-Survival level 51
    and laterality 87–88

Davies, Elizabeth 63, 125
Davies-White, Ann 179
deep breathing 50
deep pressure stimulation
    Minute Moves 29
    sensation 56, 57
    with infant feeding difficulties 4–5
depth perception 22
desk placement 78, 103, 126
developmental sequencing 33–34
Developmental Symphony 62, 73–74
dimensions of space 18, 20–23
directionality
    Angel Taps 104
    chart of behavior 100
    difficulties 99–104
    overview 18–19
    strategies for success 102
    student profile 101
dominance
    and classroom desk arrangement 126
    determining 125–126
    IMAS assessment items 163
    overview 86
Double Robo-Pats 89
Drawing 8's 91–92
drawing geometric forms 31, 159
Drum 111–112
Dryden, Gordon 119, 121

Educational Kinesiology Foundation 178
emotional-heart connection 2–3, 23
Endangered Minds 137
energy levels, monitoring 26
environment, prenatal xiii–xiv, 2–3
ergonomics
    classroom lighting 131–132

       desk placement   78, 103, 126
       and posture   67
extension
       basic extension   59–60
       butterfly extension   60
       Developmental Symphony   62, 73–74
       extension trio   61
       Superman extension   60–61
extension trio   61
eye dominance, IMAS assessment item   163
eye-hand coordination
       activities   110
       graph of scores   153, 155
       IMAS assessment item   165
       Squiggles   115–116

feeding difficulties (infant)   4
Figure 8's
       Air 8's   92
       and laterality   91–93
       ANS-Survival level   51
       Balance 8's   92
       Body 8's   80
       Drawing 8's   91–92
       Partner 8's   80
       Pointer 8's   92–93
       variations   86
       Walking 8's   91
figure-ground   78
Findeisen, Barbara   179
Five Minutes to Better Reading Skills   124, 177
focusing
       and academics   134–135
       ANS-Survival level   48–49
       difficulties   56
       figure-ground   78
       See also sensation   56
food for learning   50
foot dominance, IMAS assessment item   163
Forearm Balance   68–69
Freeman, Cecilia K.   178
From Sight to Vision   130
full-spectrum lighting   131–132

geometric forms, reproducing   31, 159
Goddard, Sally   1
Goedert, Steven
       contact information   178
       interview   130–131
Grace's story   3–6

gross motor skills
    graph of scores   154, 155
    IMAS assessment item   165

Half-Kneel Balance   71
hand dominance, IMAS assessment item   163
Hannaford, Carla
    Smart Moves   105
    The Dominance Factor   86
Harmon, Darrell   131–132
Healy, Jane M.   137
Heiniger, Margot
    Learning Tree Seminars   ix
    Pyramid of Learning   169
    The Integrated Motor Activities Screening   37, 95
    Tree of Learning 168
    tapes   179
home learning environment   142–144
hopping activities   98
How Does Your Engine Run?   45, 48
Howe, Linda   178
hyperactivity   134–135

IMAS Student Data Summary Chart   161
individualized sessions
    organizing   30, 38–41
    referring students   31–32
Infinity Walk   86
Integrated Motor Activities Screening (IMAS)
    auditory-visual-motor skills   107, 111, 155, 164
    behavior   153, 164
    body awareness 163
    case study   146–156
    dominance   163
    eye control   163
    eye-hand coordination   153, 155, 165
    gross motor skills   154, 155, 165
    IMAS assessment items   163-165
    IMAS Student Data Summary Chart   161
    Margot's One-Minute assessment   165
    Observation Sections   160
    posture 163–164
    and reading intervention   158–160
    Relationship of IMAS Items to the Learning Pyramid (chart)   162
    Scored Sections 160
    statistical case study   146–156

joint compression   29
jumping activities   95–97

Kephart, Newell C.   18, 83

kinesthetic system
    integrating   36
    overview   15
Kline, Peter   144
Knee Balance   71
Kranowitz, Carol Stock   53, 121

laterality
    chart of behavior 84
    difficulties   101
    overview   17–18
    strategies for success   86
    student profile   85
learning and the emotional-heart connection 23
learning difficulties
    listening 128–129
    vision   130–133
learning environment   142–144
Learning Pyramid
    academics   19
    ANS-Survival level   12–14
    body image   17
    chart   11
    directionality   18–19
    laterality   17–18
    overview   6–7, 12
    posture 16–17
    pre-academics   19
    sensation   15–16
    See also specific sections
Learning Tree Seminars   ix
letter reversals   102–103
lighting, classroom   131–132
Lipton, Bruce   3, 179
Listening Ears   51, 111
listening skills
    and academics   128–129
    connection to writing   128–129
    developing listening programs   128–129
    difficulties   128–129
    overview   118
listening therapy 5–6, 128–129
logistics
    classroom lighting   131–132
    desk placement   67, 78, 103, 126

Madaule, Paul   129
Margot's One-Minute assessment   165
Marsden Ball Activities
    with academics   123
    contact information   177

massage. *See* deep pressure stimulation; resistive pressure
midline difficulties
    geometric drawings as indicator   159
    overview   18
Minute Moves
    ANS-Survival level   50–51
    chart   27
    Margot's One-Minute assessment   165
    One Minute Warm-Up for Reading   28
    One Minute Warm-Up for Writing   29
    One-Minute Vision Tracking   114
    overview   26, 50–51
Morning Moves in Minutes. *See* Minute Moves
mother's feelings as part of child development   2
Motor Planning Puzzles   81–82
movement
    incorporating into academics   122–124
    movement-learning connection overview   22–26
    prenatal xiii–xiv, 2–3, 55
    Summary Chart of Movements   43–44
music, with rhythm tapping   50

neonatal flexion
    as movement   55
    See also prenatal learning
neurological fatigue break 135
New Dimensions Foundation   179

Observation Survey   146, 158
OK's   117
One Minute Warm-Up for Reading 28
One Minute Warm-Up for Writing 29
Optometric Extension Program   177
organization skills
    ANS-Survival level   48–49
    for classroom   120–121, 143–144

pace   22
palm reversals   118
Paper Crumpling (PC's)   116
parasympathetic nervous system   12–14
Parents Active for Vision Education (P.A.V.E.)   132
Partner 8's   80
Perceptual-Motor Remedial Activities and Developmental P.E. Continuum   63
Pert, Candace   12
phonics drills   124
physiological changes in nervous system   13
Pointer 8's   92–93
posture

    activities and skills   63–74
    and ergonomics 67
    chart of behavior 64
    IMAS assessment items   163–164
    overview   16–17
    strategies for success   66
    student profile 65
    for writing   29
    See also balance

pre-academics
    chart of behavior 106
    overview   19
    strategies for success   108–110
    student profile 107

prenatal learning
    as first experiences of learning   xiii–xiv, 2–3
    prenatal movement   55

pressure. See deep pressure stimulation, resistive pressure

prone vision tracking   112–113

Pyramid of Learning
    overview   12, 169
    See also Learning Pyramid

Rabbit Ears   116–117

Randolph, Shirley
    Learning Tree Seminars   ix
    Pyramid of Learning   169
    Tree of Learning 168

READ KWIK:LEARN KWIK   124, 177

reading
    connection with listening 128
    incorporating IMAS into reading intervention programs   158–160
    One Minute Warm-Up for Reading 28
    visual readiness   132–133

Record of Oral Language 146 - 147, 158

referring students
    overview   31–32
        S'cool Moves for Learning Referral   32

Regan, Freddie Ann
    contact information   178
    interview   134–135

Relationship of IMAS Items to the Learning Pyramid (chart)   162

resistive pressure 29, 68–73

reversals (letter) 102–103

rhythm 22

rhythm tapping 50

Robo-Pats
    and directionality 104
    and laterality   88–89
    Cross Crawl Robo-Pats   89
    Double Robo-Pats   89

Rocking Balance 69
rubber ball activities 123–124

SAMONAS. *See* Spectral Activate Music of Optimal Natural Structure (SAMONAS)
school learning environment 120–121, 143–144
school supplies, organizing 121
S'cool Moves for Learning
    Certificate of Participation 42
    chart of behavior 6–10
    compensating behavior 34–36
    developmental sequencing 33–34
    individualized sessions 37–44
    integrating 36
    Minute Moves 26–29, 50–51
    Minute Moves chart 27
    organizing 40–41
    program development 33
    Referral 32
    referring students 31–32
    small groups and individualized sessions overview 30, 37–44
    splinter skills 36
    student self-evaluation 35
    Summary Chart of Movements 43–44
    supporting students 35
self-evaluation, student 35
self-image, through self-portrait 31, 138–139, 159
self-portrait 31, 80, 138–139, 159
sensation
    Butterfly Legs 58–59
    Butterfly Wings 58
    chart of behavior 54
    deep pressure stimulation 29, 56, 57
    muscle sensation 29
    overview 15–16, 53–62
    skin sensation 29
    strategies for success 56
    student profile 55
    See also focusing; sensory integration difficulties
Sensing, Feeling, and Action 25
sensory integration
    and academics 134–135
    difficulties 15–17, 56
    Sensory Integration Dysfunction 121
    Sensory Integration International 179
    See also sensation
Sensory Integration Dysfunction 121
Sensory Integration International 179
sequence 22
Shellenberger, Sherry 45, 48
Sit and Pats

ANS-Survival level 51
overview 117–118
with Word Wall 122–123
Sitting Balance 71–72
skipping activities 98
skipping rope 95–97
small groups and individualized sessions
incorporating into the classroom and home 38–40
organizing 40–41
overview 30
referring students 31–32
supplies and equipment 38
Smart Moves 105
space, dimensions of space 18, 20–23
spatial relationships, and self-portraits 159
Spectral Activate Music of Optimal Natural Structure (SAMONAS) 128–129
Squiggles 115–116
Standing Balance 72
STAR Foundation 179
strategies for success
academics 121
ANS-Survival level 48–49
body image 78
laterality 86
posture 66
pre-academics 108–110
sensation 56
student profiles
academics 120
ANS-Survival level 47
Ashley 138–141
body image 77
directionality 101
Grace 3–6
laterality 85
posture 65
pre-academics 107
sensation 55
student profiles, statistical
IMAS score charts 153–156
program design 146–147
school demographics 146
School Improvement Program (SIP) 147–149
Title I 149–150
Sudden Infant Death Syndrome (SIDS) 4
Summary Chart of Movements 43–44
Sunbeck, Deborah
contact information 179
Infinity Walk 86
Superman extension 60–61
supporting students 35
Sway Balance 72–73

sympathetic nervous system 12–14
Symphony. *See* Developmental Symphony

Terry, Bonnie 177
The Coordinated Classroom 131–132
The Dominance Factor 86
The Everyday Genius 144
The Integrated Motor Activities Screening 37, 95
The Learning Revolution 24, 26, 119, 121, 136
The Out-of-Sync Child 53, 121
The Physical Side of Learning 99
The Slow Learner in the Classroom 83
Therapro 177
TherapyWorks, Inc. 179
tossing activities 118
Tree of Learning 168

vestibular system, overview 15
Vision 8's 113
vision therapy 130–133
vision tracking
    and learning difficulties 130–133
    One-Minute Vision Tracking 114
    prone 112–113
    palming 114
    Vision 8's 113
visual figure-ground 78
visual processing
    and academics 130–133
    overview 108–110
    integrating visual system 36
    readiness to read 132–133
visual-motor activities 107
Vos, Jeannette 119, 121

Walking 8's 91
water 50
When Listening Comes Alive 129
Williams, Mary Sue 45, 48
Wolff, Bruce 130
Word Wall 122–123, 124
writing
    connection with the auditory system 128–129
    difficulties 127
    and eye-hand coordination 110
    One Minute Warm-Up for Writing 29
    posture 29

yawning 109

Zion, Leela C. 99